TABLE TALK AND TIDBITS

TABLE TALK

TABLE TALK

AND TIDBITS

STORIES AND RECIPES
FROM AROUND THE WORLD

COMPILED BY DOROTHY A. STEVENS

THE JUDSON PRESS
PHILADELPHIA, PENNSYLVANIA

To my Father and Mother
who led me into the Christian fellowship
and
into an appreciation of People everywhere

By the Author
Missionary Education in a Baptist Church
Table Talk and Tidbits

Acknowledgments

Poems from the Far East. Elsie Northrup Chaney. New York: Fleming H. Revell, 1939. For quotation on page 26, "The Cook."

Good Shepherd Cook Book. Brooklyn, New York: Church of the Good Shepherd, William F. Sunday, Ph.D., Pastor, 1950. For recipe on page 74, "Chicken Noodle Soup."

The undiscovered author and publisher of the poem that appears on page 34, "Several Big Bowls." Proper acknowledgment will be made later if they should be found.

Contents

7

9

> *The pine trees on the end pieces symbolize the up-*
> *rightness of the Christian and his aspiration toward*
> *God.*

Preface

Stimulating conversation is indeed a "lost art" in many homes and organizations. As I have traveled across our country, a hobby of mine has been to make a study of conversations.

I have noticed that often the table discussion consists of relating news about certain personalities within the community, parish or denomination, the ever-present weather conditions, or information regarding local problems. I have watched with appreciation a skillful hostess, or some member of the group, guide the conversation into wider areas of religious concepts, of the application of the teaching of Jesus to modern life or to world issues. It does seem that in Christian groups, one occasionally should find informal Christian conversation as well as the more formal discussions from pulpits and lecture platforms.

The question often is asked, "But how do you do it?" Any hostess also knows this familiar question: "Where did you get the recipe for this delicious dish?"

Skillfully, the author of *Table Talk and Tidbits* has provided an answer to both questions in this very useful book.

I prophesy that it will be used not only for group meals, both large and small, and for hospitality within the home, but that it will be read by individuals for personal enrichment and for appreciation of peoples and cultures.

11

The stories and recipes interpret life in more than twenty countries around the world and a cross section of the United States. The material is planned interdenominationally, although the editor does not tell what denominations the contributors represent. This book will help toward a better understanding of the life and task of the church around the world.

We need more such creative ideas as we are trying to build a world of understanding and good will.

MRS. JAMES D. WYKER, *President*
United Church Women

New York, N. Y.
March 16, 1953

Introduction

One of the greatest privileges of my life has been the opportunity to "collect" friends—around the world, around the United States and around my world-in-a-nutshell home town, New York. What happy experiences we have shared! Many of these good times have accurred when we were eating together—a bowl of soup or a banquet, simple or exotic fare, it made little difference. The food has been remembered because of the fellowship.

In this book, it is my pleasure to tell you about fellowship and food that are the gifts of my friends. May you, too, sense their friendship as you read and eat!

In our home, we have found that acquaintances become friends about our table. It is so easy to find something in common through the simplest things. Perhaps the cups are different tonight: one came from Japan, very old; a violet one came from Holland, a third was the last cup in the store when we bought it in Canada during the war, and a hand-painted one was carried out to an American Indian field by a pioneer missionary. Which cup will you choose? A story goes with it. Our story calls for one from a newcomer at our table. Soon we are friends because we have found so much in common.

The same experience follows the use of unusual table linen. This was an Arab hunter's headdress; or the lace was made by artistic church women in Mexico; or the embroidered medallions on this cloth and napkins picture the old modes of transportation in China. Every object leads to a story of missions, and missions leads to the gospel, and the gospel makes hearts glow with unforgettable friendships in Christ.

"What wonderful food" is a natural response to any dish prepared from recipes in TABLE TALK AND TIDBITS. Then the story is ready, and a Christian conversation is launched. Of course, our friends' experiences are worth reading or telling even without the food.

Every story-recipe was written with *you* in mind, to share with you an experience and a dish surrounded by remembrance of rich Christian fellowship.

From near and far friends responded to my invitation to share a recipe and the story of a Christian experience with many others through

13

this book. The first contribution was "Good American," from a home missionary. Soon after, on one day came stories from West China, the Fiji Islands and Germany. This was in the closing days of 1950. The last response came early in 1953 from Cuba. These and all between are rich and greatly appreciated gifts from choice friends, bound to us in the family of God.

The title of the book was a gift from Florence Stansbury. She wrapped up pages of explanation in four short words. Her enthusiasm has helped me on innumerable occasions.

Mrs. James D. Wyker caught the purpose of the book and most graciously and enthusiastically prepared the preface. Thus there was added another glowing experience to this happy chain of events.

The process of producing the book has enlisted the interest of many people. Miss Alberta L. Kilmer has helped to type the manuscript and read proof; the Judson Press "family" has worked with me to make the book attractive; the artists caught and reflected the friendly spirit of the stories.

Thanks go also to those who have given permission to use quotations. The poem about the Chinese meal on page 34 came from a China missionary. She could not trace the source of the poem. I also have tried unsuccessfully to find the writer or publisher. To both go grateful appreciation.

May TABLE TALK AND TIDBITS bring many guests to your table and enrich your fellowship in Christ.

—DOROTHY A. STEVENS

AFRICA

Kintuadi Hymn

A Translation

Hold, O hold my hand,
I cannot walk alone;
Please hold it, Friend Jesus,
So that I may go the whole way.
Hold, O hold my hand,
The way is very dark,
I cannot stumble or fall
In the light of Thy face.

Kintuadi

By RHODA B. ARMSTRONG

Kintuadi (kin-twah-dee) is a very nice Kikongo word. It means fellowship. It means sharing. It means togetherness. It means that lovely feeling you have when you meet other Christians, no matter where you find them, no matter how different their race or tribe may be from yours.

Some years ago we tried an experiment in *kintuadi*. There are more than a dozen tribes represented among the Christians in the Kwango district in Congo, now served by four mission stations. Very occasionally a few of the pastors might meet each other in a conference, but the majority of the Christian workers knew only the other workers in the territory of his own mission station. So we organized a ten-day institute to which all the pastors and teachers from the mission stations, the district churches and the regional schools were invited. A few medical workers came, too. Now in America, summer assemblies and camps are well known. But in Congo it was a new venture. Much prayer and careful thought went into the preparation, with perhaps an anxious inquiry, too: How will it go? Will the people respond?

In order to make it truly indigenous, and not something done by the foreign missionaries, the institute was held in a

The bare arm represents the black man; the cuffed arm, the white man. This signifies Christian hands reaching across the seas, the churches in Congo to the churches in America.

—*Kongo Kintuadi*

native church center where all the delegates, Congolese and missionary, slept in camp style under grass-thatched roofs. Each one brought his own blankets, mosquito nets and dishes. The local church undertook to provide the meals, and each day women came from a different village to cook. Manioc flour for *luku* (a thick porridge which is the daily diet in Congo), pumpkin seeds, greens, hot red peppers, dried caterpillars—all were donated by the Christians in many villages. Hunters went out daily, and more than once the whole assembly ate wild pig or antelope.

One evening we had a *kintuadi* meeting around a big campfire; in other words, a good "get-together." To make it a real party, bananas and peanut butter cookies were passed around. Talk was lively. Questions were asked, on the part of the Congolese, about the far-off, glamorous land of America; on the part of the missionaries, about the customs and traditions of the different tribes. Many folk stories were told, each one with a point. Here are two stories actually told by Mfuta, who came from the Moanza station:

TWO OXEN

Two oxen, one white, one black, were great friends and always went around together. When they ate, they always stood back to back, and thus they could quickly spy the leopard, or any other dangerous animal, approaching. Their sharp horns made a good defense, and when they fought side by side, no one could overcome them.

But the white ox was proud, and little by little his pride began to get the better of him. "Think how beautiful I am," he would say to himself. "Why should I go around with a common black ox?" And he would wander off and begin to feed by himself.

The black ox, too, had unkind thoughts in his heart and was suspicious. "The white ox tries to get all the food for himself. He does not want me to have as much as he does," said the black ox and wandered off in a different direction in order to try to get more food for himself.

The leopard was on the alert, and as soon as the oxen were separated, he jumped on one and killed it. As soon as it was finished off, he killed the other one.

18

HEAVE HO!

A man had gone to the river to hunt and had been fortunate enough to kill a hippopotamus. But when he tried to get the huge animal out of the water, he found that it was impossible for him to do so by himself. So he called all the men in the village to come and help him, and with much excitement they all came running. They quickly prepared strong ropes made of forest vines, and fastened these around the hippo. The men got a good grip on the long vines extending out on shore and began to pull in unison:

> Heave ho! pull up our meat.
> Heave ho! our hippo comes.

And little by little the great bulk of the hippo came sliding out of the water.

> Heave ho! pull up our meat.
> Heave ho! our hippo comes.

And still farther it came up, until only a little was left in the water. Then the man who had shot the hippo cried:

> Heave ho! pull up *my* meat.
> Heave ho! *my* hippo comes.

As soon as the villagers heard that, they all dropped the rope, and with a great splash the hippo slid back into the water. The hunter realized that without the help of others, he would have no meat at all, so he cried:

> Heave ho! pull up *our* meat.
> Heave ho! *our* hippo comes.

And before too long, the hippopotamus was on shore being cut up, and there was meat enough for everybody in the village.

BELGIAN CONGO

PEANUT COOKIES

½ cup shortening
3 tablespoons peanut butter
1⅓ cups granulated sugar
2 eggs, beaten

⅔ cup chopped peanuts
⅛ teaspoon baking soda
2 cups sifted flour
¼ teaspoon salt

Cream the shortening and peanut butter together. Add sugar gradually. Add eggs, stir well. Sift flour, soda, salt, then add peanuts to this. Mix everything well. Shape in small balls, place on greased cooky sheet, press flat with bottom of small glass dipped in flour. Bake in moderate oven (400°) 10-12 minutes.

19

Prepared to Taste

By Rhoda B. Armstrong

We have suffered from a feeling of frustration. There are distinctive Congo dishes, certainly, but some of them would not be very palatable to Americans. Some of them, however, are very good, such as *mwamba nsusu*, chicken prepared in palm oil. But where in America would one get palm oil? For it is not the oil itself that is important so much as the thicker residue when the pure oil is skimmed off. No cooking fat produced in America could possibly be used as a substitute. I have known missionaries to take home a jar of palm oil in order to cook this dish at home.

Out here we make our own peanut butter. We roast the peanuts, then grind them in a meat grinder. At first they are broken into pieces which get smaller and smaller, as we continue to feed them back into the machine and regrind them. If they are ground often enough, one gets the smooth fresh-tasting peanut butter that, to our minds, beats any commercial product. If we want crunchy peanut butter, we simply save a little of the first grinding to mix in the final product. Add a little salt to make it good.

The Congolese make peanut butter, too. But they grind the peanuts on a flat stone with a rounded stone as the grinding implement. They add hot red peppers to it. They use the peanut butter to cook in certain greens, with pumpkin seeds, and sometimes with chicken.

BELGIAN CONGO

20

African Safari

By EUNICE E. DODGE

In 1948-1949 our family crossed Africa by car from Luanda, Angola, to Beira, Mozambique, and back again. In the process we stopped at nearly every Protestant mission station in our path through Angola, Belgian Congo, Northern Rhodesia, Southern Rhodesia and Mozambique. At many of the missions we were entertained overnight, or for a meal, or at least for a cup of tea.

Strange to say, the food most often produced as a treat for company was banana bread. We collected several different recipes for this delicacy as we went along. If by chance we stopped at a place where banana bread was not served, we usually left a copy of the recipe there!

21

Bananas, you see, are available in almost all parts of Africa. And the rest of the ingredients needed to make banana bread are easy to obtain, too. Many of our American sweets are difficult to make in Africa because of the lack of the proper materials. But banana bread always seems possible to make — and it never fails to please! For tea, it is just the thing. For carrying lunches along the way, it makes superb sandwiches that do not need a filling and do not dry out before time to eat them. And as a special bread to eat with dinner, "it can't be beat." Eaten hot, it doesn't go far nor last long because it cannot be sliced thin, but nobody wants a *thin* slice anyway. Eaten cold, it goes further, but everyone longs for seconds!

Right now, as I sit here writing, heart-warming memories come to me of the lovely times we have had in so many missionary homes, eating banana bread together, exchanging experiences and ideas about our work, and parting — each stronger for having fellowshiped together.

NEW JERSEY

BANANA BREAD

½ cup shortening
1 cup sugar
2 eggs

1 teaspoon soda
1 teaspoon salt
2 cups flour

3 medium bananas sliced

Cream shortening; add sugar; beat eggs and add. Beat in bananas; sift dry ingredients and add slowly. Pour into greased loaf pan and bake one hour in moderate oven.

Brave Coeur Club

By Myrta P. Ross

Peanuts or "ground nuts" are plentiful in many parts of Africa. The Congo name, *nguba,* seems to have followed the famous lowly peanuts to America where we still often hear them called "gubers." Peanuts are sold in the market place in many parts of Africa in various and varied forms. Children and grownups munch them for lunch. Peanut patties or cakes are a delicacy which African women offer with pride in their stalls at the market. Peanut oil furnishes rich cooking fat. Peanut vines are recommended fertilizer for depleted soil. Peanut milk is a substitute for cow's milk where there are no cows.

One special memory that I have of peanut loaf centers in the *Brave Coeur Club* of our African mission. The club was organized to help young married couples solve some of their problems, which were many, as they came from a polygamous culture into the monogamy of Christian marriage. A custom which the women found almost impossible at first was that of eating with their husbands. In polygamous society each woman had her own kitchen where she and her children ate, while her husband was served his food, usually with some of his male friends, in his central house in the compound where his harem lived. It was an unheard-of thing for women to eat with the men. But young African Christian men very much wanted their wives to come to the table with them to have family worship and family fellowship.

The habits of the ages are deep rooted! Young women simply could not enjoy their food if they had to eat in the presence of their husbands. So a group of courageous young couples decided to form the *Brave Coeur Club* (Brave Heart

23

Club). It would take brave hearts, indeed, for one of the plans was to have a club dinner once a month. Groups of women would take turns preparing the food. And husbands and wives would sit around a big table and eat together. Nobody could measure the agonies some of those brave hearts endured. For some it was too much. More than one came armed with a bowl from her own kitchen, and when the food was served on the plate set before her at the table, she would scrape it off in her bowl, tie the bowl up in a kerchief, and sit waiting to carry it home when the party broke up. There in the privacy of her kitchen the party delicacies would be enjoyed! Even when peanut loaf was on the menu!

But time and experience remove prejudices and break down customs and mores. Courage did spread from one brave heart to another until there came to be, on the mission station, a sizable company of young couples who found their family life developing around the table in the home even as the life of the church was developing around the table of our Lord.

NEW YORK

PEANUT LOAF

2 cups cooked rice	1½ cups milk
2 cups peanuts, ground fine	2 teaspoons salt
3 eggs	pinch of pepper

Mix the cooked rice and ground peanuts. Beat the eggs slightly. Add milk gradually to the eggs. Combine milk, eggs, rice and peanuts. Add salt and pepper. Put into a greased loaf baking pan. Bake in a moderate oven (350°). Serve with a cream white sauce or cheese sauce. This is a good meat substitute.

ASIA

The Cook

It is a pleasant task I have each morn
And as I sweep the dusty ground, I smile.
I push three sticks between three stones, whereon
I place my cooking pot, and in a while
There comes to me the sound of bubbling rice.

I smile. For on the morrow, rice shall be
A man's strong muscle reaping harvest grain;
A child's gay laughter, running home to me
For food. The miracle is God's again;
My hand and cooking pot, His loved device.

—ELSIE NORTHRUP CHANEY

Snake Steak!

By Genevieve S. Sowards

In Bassein, Burma, whenever people came from America, especially our mission secretaries, we always had a station dinner, all of the missionaries in our three separate mission centers in Bassein coming together at one of the mission houses.

This particular dinner was at Dr. Nichols' house, and fifteen of us were sitting around the big, extended table. Our Karen girls were helping the Indian cooks by serving. At such occasions, there was true fellowship, and we put aside the weightier problems and matters of the mission and had a time of light conversation — and sometimes tall tales. Often the conversation got around to snake stories. Every missionary has his favorite snake story. After one story, Miss Tingley said:

"Oh, that's nothing. A big snake (measuring with her hands) was killed this very afternoon just outside my dining-room doors."

"That big!" our guest from America exclaimed. "What did you do with it?"

"Oh, I didn't worry about that," Miss Tingley shrugged. "It was an edible kind."

"Edible! You mean to say that people eat snakes?" He nearly rose out of his chair in amazement.

I noticed that the girls serving table left quickly. From where I sat, I could see them put down the serving dishes in the pantry-porch and then double up with silent laughter. You see, it was they who had cleaned the snake, cut up the thick steaks of the back muscles and made them into delicious curry — they say. But we poor missionaries were serving our honored guests from America curry made from everyday meat. BURMA

Curry

By GENEVIEVE S. SOWARDS

Curry is not a specific dish but is rather a class of foods, as a stew, so called because of its seasoning of curry powder. Curry powder is a yellow, spicy powder, containing turmeric, spices, seeds and chillies. Native cooks of Burma usually buy these ingredients separately and pulverize and mix them according to their tastes. The curries of different lands and peoples vary characteristically according to the proportions of the different ingredients in the curry powder. American and Indian and British spice companies put out ready-prepared curry powder, but it does not taste "like home."

"Rice and curry" is the food of Burma, India, Malaya. It is eaten all year, every day, every meal, by all classes. Rice is the food; curry is what goes with it. They always say "rice and curry," as we say "bread and butter."

The ingredients of curry can, in truth, be almost anything. Some of the people of Burma put into curry things which we do not eat. A well-educated Burmese man once told me that red-ant curry was very delicious. The muscles of snakes, frogs and field rats are eaten. Other meats are beef, pork, mutton, deer, chicken and other fowl — tame and wild — game, fish and shrimps. Eggs are used — chicken, duck and turtle. Vegetable curries are not as popular as meat curries, but vegetables are often combined with meat. *Dahl* is the cheapest kind of curry. It is made of *dahl,* like yellow split peas, with onions, fat and curry powder. Other vegetables used in curries are potatoes, green beans, cabbage, cauliflower, tomatoes, celery.

The foods are cooked in a stew, highly and brightly seasoned with yellow curry powder. Most curry recipes in

American cookbooks have too little curry powder to be really called curry. The people of Burma who like very hot foods often add hot chillies and green ginger. Fresh grated coconut and coconut milk are usually added. Sesame oil and peanut oil are often used for fat.

The Burmese way of eating curry is with one's fingers. The rice, cooked dry and fluffy, and the curry with the liquid cooked down are mixed together neatly in a little ball for each bite. The fingers are not dirtied above the first joints. The little ball is held by the fingertips with the thumb behind it to pop it into the mouth. It is daintily and expertly done, and is really an art — as you will discover when you try it. Or use the English way of eating curry, with a dessert or tablespoon in the right hand and a fork in the left, used to help break up pieces of meat and to push the food into the spoon.

Rice and curry is a meal in itself, but various condiments or relishes are often served with it. Some are: peanuts coarsely ground, crisp fried onions, tomatoes and coconut finely chopped together, grated hard-boiled egg, ground pickles or relish, spiced grated pineapple, chopped green peppers or chopped green peppers and raw onions.

Bananas often are eaten with curry — skinned and put on the plate and cut and eaten with the spoon. In serving, pass the rice first, then the curry, and then the condiments.

BURMA

Karen Association

By Genevieve S. Sowards

"Association" is the big topic of conversation in a Karen village a whole year before it is host to four or five thousand people for three or four days. It takes much planning and hard work for a little jungle village to feed and care for so many. Being host, according to Karen hospitality tradition, means feeding all of the visitors free. Every family in a Karen Christian village, according to plans worked out ahead of time, raises more rice, more pigs, more chickens — for the Association.

The actual Association time arrives. Thousands of guests are greeted and made to feel welcome. They sleep in large bamboo and thatch dormitories made especially for this occasion. A large *mandat* or bamboo-supported, rice-straw-covered auditorium is the main meeting place. Rice straw thickly covers the ground where the people sit. There is a platform with chairs for the speakers.

During Association, the women cook almost all the time. They cannot cook enough for everyone at the same time and so they cook giant pot after pot, over open wood fires. As there is no refrigeration and it is hot, pigs have to be butchered the day they are eaten. Chickens, fish and vegetables have to be prepared by the hundreds.

When a pot of rice as big as a washtub is done, word is passed along and a line forms. Children come running, and the older ones compliment the cooks on the best curry in the world. Each guest is given a large square of new silky banana leaf which he holds in his open palm. On it is heaped fluffy steaming rice and over it is poured yellow, spicy curry. Each guest finds himself a place to squat, according to native custom. There he eats his delicious meal from his banana leaf, using his fingers, expertly, neatly, according to prescribed Burmese table manners. Dishwashing is no problem!

Tremendous as the task is to feed so many with almost no equipment, these Karen women laugh and chat at their work and scoop out food for their guests as graciously as any western woman serves at a crystal-linen-and-silver banquet table.

BURMA

RICE AND CURRY

A cup of uncooked rice will make about three cups of cooked rice. Allow one-half cup uncooked rice for each person. Wash the rice thoroughly. Put the rice in boiling water. Stir it to be sure that it circulates freely in plenty of water. Boil uncovered until the water *begins* to get milky. Drain off the water and return to the fire—very low. Steam, uncovered, until done. Never stir with a spoon. Use a two-prong fork to stir or fluff-up the rice as it steams in a heavy aluminum pan. If the fire is very low and the rice is steamed for an hour or so, the rice on the bottom of the pan will be browned —dry and hard—and is the best part. It is delicious with butter and brown sugar. Serve both brown and fluffy white rice.

CURRY

1 pound ground beef, or beef or pork, cut in small pieces	Salt
	Chili powder
1 tablespoon lard or vegetable shortening	4 stalks celery
	½ cup tomato juice
1 large onion	½ cup water
1 tablespoon curry powder, or more if you like	

If ground meat is used, make into small balls. Fry in fat until brown. Add chopped onion. Fry the onion a little. Add tomato juice and water. Add celery cut in small pieces, including the leaves. Add any other vegetables that you may have, fresh or left over. The same vegetables can be used as are used in vegetable soup. Keep a relative proportion of each. Add salt and curry powder. If you want curry hotter, add Mexican chili powder. Cook until done. Serve with rice.

31

Bowl After Bowl

By LETTIE G. ARCHER

I am faced with the sad fact that I shall not be able to return to China, but my dear Chinese friends there are daily in my thoughts. Just today, as I plan to serve a Chinese meal to some of my American friends, I recall some of the last feasts before furlough, and especially the faces and personalities of those who ate with me.

I think there could be nothing more sociable than a Chinese feast. The meal consists in bowl after bowl of their specialties, one bowl for each course. The bowl is put in the center of the table and the guests help themselves from it with chopsticks at the invitation of the host or hostess. The distance of each guest from the bowl, therefore, cannot be far. This means that but eight or ten may sit at a table. Thus the guests are brought together in a very homey way. Conversation becomes intimate, and we spend a truly delightful hour together.

What wouldn't I give to sit down with those dear Chinese friends again, especially to eat that most delectable dish, chicken and peanuts, or *je din,* as they call it. I hope that each group that prepares this dish will offer a prayer that the beautiful Christian fellowship we enjoyed in those days will strengthen all of us through every day.

CHINA

JE DIN—chicken and peanuts

Bone one large chicken. Cut into one-third inch cubes.

One hour before serving, turn into a frying pan with four tablespoons of piping hot melted fat. Constantly turn with a ladle or spatula until chicken is seared a light brown. Add soy sauce until it is sufficiently salted to suit your taste. Sprinkle generously with black pepper. Add a cup of diced red mangoes. Then add water sufficient to let it simmer and still have some juice left when tender.

Dissolve a tablespoon of cornstarch in water. Stir into juice enough to thicken it just slightly.

When ready to serve, add a pint of peanuts, and turn immediately into a bowl for serving.

The bony parts of the chicken and some surplus fat could be used to make a kettle of broth in which meat balls could be cooked. This would make a second dish. The two, with steamed rice, should serve a group of eight, the basis of any Chinese meal.

A New Christmas Celebration

Chinese Church Family Dinner

By MINNIE ARGETSINGER

December 20, 1947: The pastor of the Chengtu Baptist Church announced a new kind of celebration commemorating the birth of Jesus. It would be a special observance and in the form of a feast.

Pastor Fuh Gin Pei's aim was to have the church members of a family attend as a unit and sit together. The family idea appealed to almost everyone. And to have the feast at Christmas added a peculiar, once-a-year kind of anticipation.

All were very much interested as the mention of a feast in China recalls delight. Each one would remember a great variety of sauces, gravies, condiments and special seasonings which make eating an enjoyment and dining an art in China.

This announcement meant different things to different people. To the more fortunate ones it meant:

> "Several big bowls on a big round table
> Steaming odors rising in a cloud
> Chopsticks clinking as the guests reach for-
>   ward
> Plucking at the duck
> Wishing for better luck
> When a bone gets stuck

Coughing as they turn around looking on
    the floor
Watching lines of cooks bringing new dishes
    in the door.

"Bird's nest soup — and chicken in a stew
Mushrooms — shellfish and shark's fins —
    shrimps
Meat balls — toasted rice and sea slugs — eels
Bamboo tips — watermelon pits
Crackling in the lips
Garlic — kidneys — pigeon eggs — fresh
Walnuts in a sweet sauce — ham and water cress."

To others it meant much less but to all alike it brought
anticipation of a joyful occasion, for never had such an occasion
been observed.

At last December twenty-fifth arrived. About eleven o'clock
the families began to come and were escorted to the reception
room, a happy meeting place.

How attractive the children looked! The children of pro-
fessional men — the University professors, physicians, dentists
and others — were gaily dressed; their short black hair and
snappy brown eyes were the center of attraction with children
of other church members who also were dressed in their best.
Each child, in a most delightful impromptu manner, would sing
or act out something he or she had learned at school. They
amused the families for quite some time.

Meanwhile the kindergarten room was being changed into
a dining room. Round tabletops were rolled in and set on
wooden horses. Usually there are certain rules concerning the
number of people sitting at a table, but today guests were
crowded together and more places had to be prepared.

Fragrant odors began to permeate the reception room and
we all joined in ohs and ahs in anticipation of good food and
fun at the tables. At last everything was ready, and Mr. Fuh

35

came to invite us to the kindergarten room. He was all smiles as he told us the food was very poor and the tables very rough. We in turn told him the food was delicious and the furniture the very best.

The members of the different families were excited to see which table was the best. They were told all equal, no high, no low, because Christians are all equal.

Mr. Fuh offered the blessing, followed by "Praise God from whom all blessings flow," sung by everyone.

On the tables were specially prepared black watermelon seeds. No feast is a feast without these. To break open the seeds is an art. One must be cracked at the proper end and then the two halves open up and the kernel easily can be extracted. This course provides an opportunity for friends to chat while the cooks are preparing the meats and vegetables.

A Chinese feast is well ordered. Dishes are presented according to their regular order.

In this feast the cold dishes were placed on the table first. They consisted of cold meats of all kinds, sliced *very* thin to make it easier to pick up with the chopsticks.

Then hot dishes were brought in at the proper time and set in the center of the table. At the signal of the host we all raised our chopsticks and tackled the food which was before us, all dipping into the same dish.

The fish, which is a popular item, had been cooked whole. It was seasoned with ginger-soya sauce, a sweet taste. It was delicious and it was not long before one side of the fish was picked clean and, by a clever act, it was turned over.

For one course a whole duck was offered to us, and again we were told not to hesitate to use our chopsticks.

Many were the dishes brought in, and especially good ones were placed at one side of the table so the guests could dip into them any time.

The vegetables in West China are many and varied. Each vegetable was combined with another and meat, cut into small pieces, was added. No one but a Chinese could concoct such delightful and delicious combinations, so delicate in flavor and so well-balanced in food values.

Toward the end of the meal the fluffy white rice was served, but we could not eat much of this.

The last article of food was a plate of cut and quartered oranges. These are delightful.

By this time the children were ready to leave the table, quite a polite custom in China.

A cup of water finally was given to each guest for him to rinse the mouth.

How much we enjoyed this great family feast and the privilege of such fine Christian fellowship!

CHINA

PEAS, CHINESE STYLE

1 cup meat cut in very small
pieces

½ teaspoon minced onion
3 thin slices ginger (fresh)

1 teaspoon brown sugar

Fry these together in fat until meat is nicely browned and nearly done.

¾ cup liquid from the peas
3 tablespoons soy sauce
⅓ cup slivered pimentos

1 can drained peas
1 pound fresh peas
Thickening

Add these and cook together until done. Serve hot with rice.

FISH

Add some Chinese soy sauce and vinegar to a cup of water. Add to this a piece of pounded fine ginger or garlic. If the fish is being fried or baked, the above is poured over it and, at frequent intervals, it is dipped over the fish.

Christianizing the Home Party

By L. EMMA BRODBECK

The last week in October, in our churches in China, is always celebrated as "Christianizing the Home" week. This program began more than twenty years ago. When I think back over all the special meetings we have had during these years, it seems there should be more to show for the effort. Perhaps we expect to do too much in one week. We always plan to continue to emphasize the home but fail to concentrate on it. There are, however, some worthwhile gains.

We have had several meetings with the members of the Canadian Mission Church, union meetings at their church and at ours. Our pastor had used "Home and Family" subjects for all his sermons in October. But the big special day of the week was a party we held on Wednesday. Perhaps you might like to give such a party at home, using the type of makeshift things we do here, and I hope you could have as good a time.

It was an invitation affair. Only families were invited, where several were regular attendants or members. We did not include our young school pupils or teachers except when they were members of Christian families. We made attractive invitations, mimeographed on the back of clean paper cut from the used greeting cards which many of you so kindly send us. There was a picture of a family and a neatly written invitation. On the envelopes we pasted pictures of a flower, also cut from used greeting cards, and it made the cheap little envelopes look quite festive. We planned for work, play, worship and food, telescoping the activities of a Christian family for a day into our two-hour party time.

We urged that families should come as units. For the games

we planned those that could be played by the whole family together. Even though we had many older people not in the habit of playing games, almost everyone played some of them.

In our games, we used simple things, most of which could be found or easily made in any home. We threw beanbags into a wash basin, with circles marked around it on the floor for lower scores. We put a walnut on a bottle and had folks walk past quickly, with arm outstretched to try to flip it off. Even the most timid will try that because they cannot understand why the others have not been able to do it.

One special game that old and young played was composed of two cones made of paper and hung on strings held taut by two players. The others had to blow the cones from one end of the string to the other. We began as a relay race between different families but later used just two contestants as new people came into the room.

After this game, they went into the next room where materials were provided for making cones to take home, to introduce the game to their neighbors. We had cut the cones from old magazines and, to make them look festive, had prepared red and blue paper triangles to paste on them. That was our work period. Everyone seemed happy to go home carrying a couple of paper cones strung on some string.

For our food, instead of having the usual tea and cakes, we decided to have stew and buns. Many of those families did not have quite enough to eat, and meat is always a treat. The meat and vegetables gave nourishment and seemed very appropriate for a raw, cold, wet day, and really were not much more expensive than a few cookies and tea.

My cook began baking buns before daylight, while my goat boy and the Canadian women's servants spent the day chopping meat and vegetables. It was worth the work. There were about 180 present; each had a big bowl of stew, then a bowl of thinner soup, and each had two or three buns. We baked 380, and all disappeared. Some folks managed to get a few to take to members of their family who could not come.

Of course, we didn't try to seat that number of people. They stood around tables that had been prepared with bowls and chopsticks.

The games and food were in the Canadian women's house. Then we went across the street to their church for our worship service. We sang the 117th Psalm which we all learned for use in the Home Week meetings. Then a layman spoke — briefly, simply, clearly and very effectively. And everybody listened. Even with all those children and the church crowded to overflowing, it was quiet and orderly. Either we had tired them out with games or filled them too full of soup for utterance, or else — How glad I am! — the children of Christian families have learned to behave in church! That is no mean accomplishment in twenty years, when one thinks of the disorder in other meetings.

At the close, all grandparents were given pictures from magazine covers. And every person there was given a picture

from a greeting card. The grownups appreciated them more than the children, for they do not have as many chances to earn rewards as do the Sunday school children. If you should try giving such a party, don't forget the picture card to take home, and tell folks to paste them on the wall to beautify their homes.

CHINA

HONG SHAO NIU RU—red braised beef stew

Ingredients	For 150	For 50	Family Dish
Stew beef	35 pounds	12 pounds	1½ pounds
Suet	2 cups	½ cup	2 table-
Vegetable oil	2 cups	½ cup	spoons
Soy sauce (and salt)	6 cups	2 cups	⅓ cup
Carrots	15 pounds	5 pounds	
Turnips	15 pounds	5 pounds	total of
Potatoes	15 pounds	5 pounds	2½ pounds
Parsley	3 bunches	1 bunch	
Celery	3 bunches	1 bunch	to flavor
Onions	1 pound	4 ounces	1 small
Ginger, raw	¼ pound	1 small root	1 inch square
Molasses	1½ cups	½ cup	2 teaspoons
Red pepper	½ pound or less	¼ pound or less	to taste

Cut the beef into chunks about 1½ inches square. Mix the soy sauce and salt into the meat; then put into the hot melted suet and vegetable oil and fry until very brown and almost dry. Then add carrots, turnips and potatoes (cut small), and brown. Add enough boiling water to simmer until meat is very tender. Add parsley and celery, onions and flavorings (molasses, ginger, red pepper). Use soy bean starch or cornstarch for slightly thicker consistency.

Serve in bowls with chopsticks, if possible.

Fresh buns make a good accompaniment, or serve with rice.

This is a typical Chinese dish. We have worked out amounts with our Chinese cook, for two large groups and for a family meal. Some of the flavors we use have no English equivalent and cannot be bought in the States, so we didn't include them. Americans will not miss them and may enjoy the dish better without them.

Unto the Hills

By DOROTHY G. GATES

One of the great joys of missionary service in China comes from the various opportunities for informal fellowship with our Chinese Christian colleagues. Life at our hospital was busy for all of us, and for our Woman's Division superintendent and doctors often close to a twenty-four-hour responsibility. One form of relaxation which was possible very occasionally was to go out several miles from the city to the place we called "the country hospital," the building which had been our refuge during air raids early in the last war. Lack of staff and the passing of the emergency need for this hospital extension reduced its function to that of storehouse, although we had visions of far greater usefulness for this building later.

One morning three of us walked out to our country hospital to rest and to renew strength and inspiration as we lifted our eyes to the hills and fellowshiped together. Toward noon our Chinese colleague prepared a simple Chinese meal such as we always enjoyed so much. It was interesting to watch her cook, and then, of course, more interesting to eat together — sitting in the open outside of the simple mud building, the rice fields and river before us and the hills beyond. With our common tasks of Christian service and lives lived together at work and at play, always seeking to glorify our Lord in all we do, how can we help but feel that "oneness of the spirit" in Christ?

One of my favorite dishes, that I learned to make that day, was Egg *Chiao-tzes*, one of several simple meat and vegetable dishes eaten with rice. The dishes, one of each kind, were in the center of the table, and each person had his bowl of rice and helped himself as he pleased.

CHINA

EGG CHIAO-TZES—filled pancakes

3 eggs
1 tablespoon flour
2 tablespoons water
½ teaspoon salt
1 tablespoon soy sauce

Beat well until smooth. Drop into hot frying pan or griddle to form "pancakes" about four inches in diameter.

CENTER MIXTURE—Chop fine:

½ cup cooked chicken, pork, fish
1 tablespoon onion
2 tablespoons cabbage
1 tablespoon celery

Fry this mixture over a hot fire for a few minutes to heat thoroughly and partially cook the raw vegetables. Do not cook until they lose all their crispness. Add one tablespoon to center of each egg pancake while hot, seal edges with a bit of raw egg, and fold in half.

Tidbits

By HELEN A. GODDARD

NUT BREAD

1 cup walnuts, cut fine
1 cup raisins
4 cups flour
4 teaspoons baking powder
1 teaspoon salt
½ cup sugar
1 egg
2 cups milk

Let rise half an hour. Bake in bread tins about one hour in moderate oven. Makes delicious sandwiches cut thin and lightly buttered, attractive for tea.

P'LAO—spiced chicken

Put half a cup of Crisco in frying pan, fry chicken (cut up) until brown, then put chicken in kettle and add water to cover. Add salt. Tie in a cheesecloth one stick cinnamon, whole cloves, twelve cardamom seeds and add to water, also half a cup raisins. Cook slowly until chicken is tender. Remove chicken, but leave raisins and spices. Put two cups of rice into the liquid, cook soft, dry in oven for a few minutes, then serve chicken with rice on top. Put spices on top. Add fried onions; also toasted almonds or peanuts.

CHINA

New Year Sweets

By Carol A. Schaefer

One of my happy memories of a glimpse into Chinese life occurred several weeks before the Chinese New Year season. One of the ladies from our church invited me to come and see her family preparing its refreshments of sweets that would be served to the many callers who, according to Chinese custom, would come to pay respects at the Chinese New Year time.

We turned off the street into a small cotton-selling shop, and went to the rear of the store; then through the back workrooms where cotton was processed, and finally reached the living quarters of the family. Actually, several families of brothers lived together, as this was the old family home; so there was a great number of cousins, sisters and aunts, all busy in the kitchen.

Some were heating syrup in a large kettle on the stove. Others were preparing the puffed rice, peanuts and sesame seeds and puffed sweet potato strips which would be mixed in the syrup. When all the ladies were satisfied that the syrup was cooked just enough, it was mixed with the various combinations of puffed rice and other good things and spread on boards. Then it was pressed down, cut and, finally, the children wrapped it in brown rice paper and stored it away in empty kerosene tins to keep fresh in that damp climate.

It was as gay and happy an occasion as our own Christmas cooky-baking day!

CHINA

T'SAO MI T'ANG—puffed rice candy

It is so hard to work out Chinese recipes and make them sound sensible in terms of American substitutes and measurements! However, it is fun to try. Here is a popular way of making puffed-rice candy.

It is a custom in China to call on all your friends at the time of the Chinese New Year. Wherever you go, sweetmeats and tea are served. *T'sao Mi T'ang* is one of the favorites and is made in large quantities to serve the many guests who call during the holiday season. It is stored in old five-gallon kerosene tins in West China to protect it from the dampness!

¼ cup butter	5 cups Rice Krispies
½ pound marshmallows	1 cup peanuts
¼ cup sesame seed	

Cook butter and marshmallows over boiling water until syrupy, stirring frequently. Put Rice Krispies in a large greased bowl and add peanuts and sesame seed. Pour the melted marshmallow syrup over this. Stir briskly. Press into a greased, shallow pan. When cool, cut into strips about three inches long and narrow, one inch thick. Wrap strips in wax paper, then bright tissue paper.

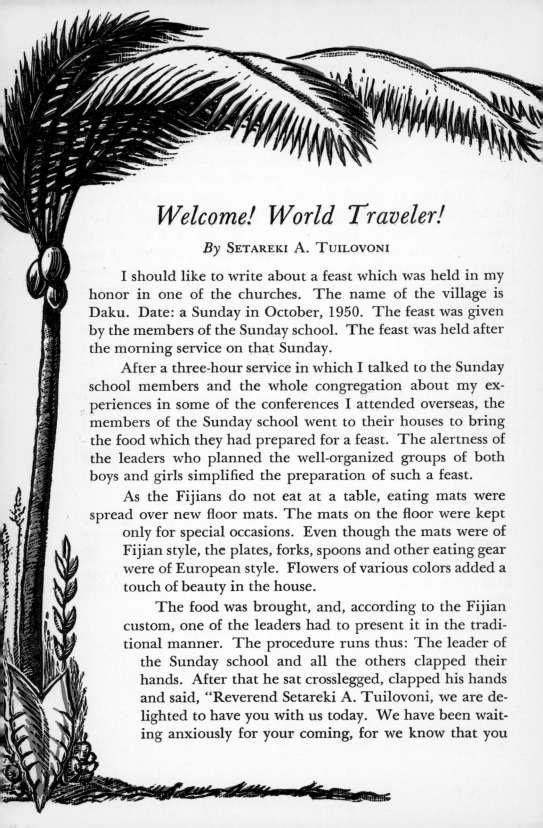

Welcome! World Traveler!

By Setareki A. Tuilovoni

I should like to write about a feast which was held in my honor in one of the churches. The name of the village is Daku. Date: a Sunday in October, 1950. The feast was given by the members of the Sunday school. The feast was held after the morning service on that Sunday.

After a three-hour service in which I talked to the Sunday school members and the whole congregation about my experiences in some of the conferences I attended overseas, the members of the Sunday school went to their houses to bring the food which they had prepared for a feast. The alertness of the leaders who planned the well-organized groups of both boys and girls simplified the preparation of such a feast.

As the Fijians do not eat at a table, eating mats were spread over new floor mats. The mats on the floor were kept only for special occasions. Even though the mats were of Fijian style, the plates, forks, spoons and other eating gear were of European style. Flowers of various colors added a touch of beauty in the house.

The food was brought, and, according to the Fijian custom, one of the leaders had to present it in the traditional manner. The procedure runs thus: The leader of the Sunday school and all the others clapped their hands. After that he sat crosslegged, clapped his hands and said, "Reverend Setareki A. Tuilovoni, we are delighted to have you with us today. We have been waiting anxiously for your coming, for we know that you had represented the Sunday schools of Fiji in the World Council of Christian Education in Toronto. We know that you will bring to us greetings from other parts of the world represented in that great Conference. To show our appreciation for your coming to us, we have decided to entertain you with this feast. Even though it is not worthy of your task, yet it is done with a Christian spirit, and we hope that you will look favorably on us."

After that I clapped my hands and replied, "It is a privilege to be with you, to tell you of the conference which I have attended. I am more than grateful to you for your interest in the work of Sunday school and other church activities. I also count it a privilege to partake of this food which you have prepared for us. I know that you have done this as a symbol of the generosity of God to us."

I then clapped my hands, the grace was said by one of the girls, and we proceeded. Two groups of young people sang hymns while others ate. The sumptuous dinner was made more significant by the harmonious singing of the young people. When they came to the mat to have their dinner, others took their places. It was an experience of joy and happiness and at the same time it was tinctured with reverence.

FIJI ISLANDS

COCONUT CREAMED FISH

A fresh fish is cleaned and fried in a frying pan.

Two or three coconuts are scraped into a basin; one cup of water is poured into the basin of coconut and mixed with it. Then the meat of the coconut is taken out leaving a liquid which looks like cow's milk. The liquid is put in a pot and heated until it begins to boil. The fish is put in the pot, with salt enough to give taste; cut tomatoes and put them in; onions and a little bit of pepper are added. Cook the fish for ten or fifteen minutes more before use.

The broth is dished out and taken before the fish is eaten.

Yams, sweet potatoes, potatoes and taro are eaten with it.

High Favorite

By Grace Howard

I must have been hungry for I woke this morning thinking about food, Indian food to be exact. My thoughts were along this line: "Why don't they . . . ?" and I foresaw the day when food packagers would be putting out Indian dinners complete in one little package that could be bought at the corner grocery, *my* corner grocery, not some fancy place in New York! You can buy Chinese dinners, so why not Indian! And, of course, I foresaw that the packagers would get the great idea from the page in the *American* headed, "Why don't they," from a paragraph I would send in, and maybe, in addition to the dinners I would soon be able to buy, the *American* might send me a small check with which to buy them!

From long years' residence in India our family has grown to appreciate Indian cookery and to think that a well-made chicken or prawn curry is a truly royal dish. But for its utmost enjoyment one does not set out the best dishes and silver and linen. The partakers should sit cross-legged on the floor, barefoot of course. In front of one, the table, tablecloth and plate are all provided in one simple article, a large piece of fresh green banana leaf about the size of a tray cloth. A glass of water is placed at

one's left hand, and a small amount of salt is placed somewhere at one edge of the leaf. Even if the hands are clean, the hostess brings a finger bowl and towel and performs a gracious little ceremony herself.

There are as many ways of cooking curry as there are of cooking stew, for curry is essentially a stew with — to us — mysterious flavorings. Also there are as many ways of choosing and combining spices and flavorings as there are cooks! When it comes to chicken curry, it is hard to say which is the best recipe or where I have eaten the most delicious dish of it. Since Indian cooks, like some good Americans, cook by rule of thumb, adding, as the mood inspires them, "a little of this and a little of that," the recipes vary from time to time.

Years ago when our family was growing up in India (our family of four curry-loving sons), we sometimes were invited to visit a friend who was and still is one of the judges in a high court. Perhaps his cook was better trained than ours, and of course better paid, and his local market afforded a better line of ingredients. For this reason, old Beroo's curry was a thing to look forward to, and now, after years, to look back upon almost with drooling! In a recent letter the judge wrote, "My old cook is still with me. He is getting no younger and has to have a jinrickshaw to take him to market each day. But he's a faithful old rogue, and I forgive him much — he's been with me since 1926."

One day the judge thought I ought to teach Beroo to make American apple pie. Armed with my pie recipe I invaded the cook's domain — there's no less word for it, for he reigned there supreme over his cookery and his youthful assistants, as many as he could wangle from the judge. One of them cooked and fed the dogs. Another washed pots and pans — the domain was highly departmentalized!

The judge's flat was on the third floor of an apartment house and directly opposite the apartment of one of the United States consuls. Their cooks exchanged black looks and belligerently borrowed this and that as necessity arose.

49

This is the recipe I obtained in exchange for apple pie. I watched the process and wrote down what I saw and heard:

"Well, lady, you first get a chicken from the market. And clean it, of course. And cut it up, of course. According to the number of people you wish to feed, buy your chicken; you may need more than one, but this is a one-chicken curry we are making today."

The chicken had recently been lying squawking on the floor at his feet, its legs tied with a red string. Now one of the boys killed and cleaned it, so that stage was out of the way.

Scattered about in leaf-wrappings — there are very few paper bags or even newspapers used for such things in India — were various spices, and a thing which looked like a small tombstone lying flat on the floor. Beside it lay a rough stone cylinder reminding one of the cylinders one sees in archaeological museums. That was the "rolling pin" with which the spices were ground to paste on the tombstone. One of the boys squatted down and began to roll vigorously, putting a few spices of each separate kind on the stone, crushing them a little and then adding a few drops of water now and then to keep them from scattering. With much elbow grease they finally were turned into a paste, and each separate spice-paste was put in its own place on the edge of a plate.

In my notebook I wrote: "*postu dana,* a little more; *gira; dhunia,* less; *haldia* — of each about one teaspoon," referring to the paste. "Two or three small onions; five beads of garlic, a small teaspoon ground (bruised) fresh root of ginger; one teaspoon of small hot chillies — not ground." The above are all called "hot spices." The following are called "warm spices": "cinnamon, a little; *elachi,* a little; one or two bay leaves, coconut water."

Now I must translate and give the method.

I knew all these spices by sight and by smell, but when I came to America I did not know what to ask for at the store in English. I used to ask to smell the jars and buy by smell, until a dear Indian friend came to visit us. He wrote down the English equivalents.

Take of the paste, or the ground powder as it is obtained here, poppy seed — a little more than one teaspoon, cumin seed, turmeric, coriander — a little less than one teaspoon.

Put four tablespoons of cooking fat, any preferred kind (Beroo used clarified butter), into a shallow saucepan. While it is heating, bruise or finely slice the onion and garlic. Add to the fat and fry slowly till a golden brown — the peppers may be added a little later out of con-

50

sideration for your eyes! Remove most of the onion and save for garnishing at serving time.

Into the fat now put the ground spices. Fry a little, to remove the raw taste. Add pieces of chicken from approximately a two pound fowl, cut somewhat as we do for stewing or frying. The chicken must be fried a little in this spicy mixture and well coated with it. Add about a pint of water, and, before the lid is put on for the whole to simmer, put in the "warm spices" also: "cinnamon, a little" (one 3-inch stick broken in small pieces); *elachi,* cardamom seeds, broken from the husk and added in, slightly bruised, husk and all, about four or five should suffice; cloves, whole, about five; and one or two bay leaves. Salt to taste.

Let it cook together, adding more water as needed so the final result will be a thickish gravylike liquid which is not to be thickened with flour as some American recipes recommend. As the chicken approaches tenderness — this will be a longer period for an Indian chicken I'm sure — and the liquid is quite reduced, the final ingredient is to be added.

The final ingredient is the thing that makes all the difference in the world, to my thinking. I have never seen it explained in an American cookbook. These adapted recipes called for "coconut milk" or "coconut water," but the orthodox method of preparation is this: Get a fresh coconut. Break it. Throw away the liquid that we call "water." Scrape the meat out with a scraper or grater. The Indians have invented some really useful graters, and it takes only a matter of minutes for them to do this. You do not laboriously break out the meat previous to grating, but hold the half coconut against the grater and scrape with a rotary motion, or, if of another type, something like a fork with the tines curved into a wide clawing surface, "claw" it out. If it is a very large coconut, you may not need all of the meat — one learns by experience. Put all the grated meat into a bowl. Pour at least one cupful of *boiling water* over it. Let stand a little, then knead and squeeze the shreds until you have extracted as much of the creamy liquid as possible. Pour this off into a cup. Now pour another cup of boiling water onto the shreds and knead and squeeze as before. You will get another cup of "milk" though not as rich as the first. This is called the "second draw," while the other is called the "first draw." If the water needs replenishing on the chicken, now is the time to add the *second* draw of coconut "milk" (the dry and tasteless shreds are thrown away), which should cook until the chicken is really done. Now, at the last, the crowning glory, the "first draw of milk" is added, much as we add butter, after which there is no more cooking or the oil will separate, and the looks as well as taste will be spoiled. Let it mix well and simmer for a bit. This curry then is served on great mounds of fluffy rice on those banana leaf plates waiting in front of hungry guests — ourselves, I hope! And, sans silver-ware, it must be lovingly conveyed to our mouths with our fingers!

As most people already know how to cook rice, I do not repeat a recipe for it. I forgot to say, though, that potatoes cut in rather large pieces, say like walnuts, may be added to the curry at a time to finish cooking with the chicken. I prefer it this way as it reduces the richness of the pure chicken curry.

All of the above sounds very complicated, but actually it isn't at all after one has assembled the required materials. The various spices can be procured at tea and coffee companies, I find, sometimes whole and sometimes even powdered. Curry powder also can be bought in most stores, though it has a far different taste when freshly ground or "pasted." Fresh ginger root is the one thing I can't get in this part of the country. Some people substitute the powdered ginger familiar to us all, but the taste isn't quite authentic.

To complete such a dinner one needs a chutney, and a lentil dish. Yellow split peas make a satisfactory lentil substitute. Cook down as for a thick soup, flavor with onion, a little turmeric, a bit of bay leaf, salt and a little sugar. There is a variety of desserts to choose from, but to me the one essential dessert is several sodamint tablets!

A year ago our youngest Indian-born son married an Indian-born girl. After the honeymoon and before they started on their journey back to school, their one special request in the way of food was for a "lickin' good old chicken curry." As nearly as possible I followed Beroo's directions for the best curry any of us had ever eaten. Perhaps one has to be born in India really to appreciate such a dish, but genuinely to like curry of any kind is to demonstrate kinship with an Indian of any kind anywhere.

INDIA

52

A Farewell Party

By Vimala Rajamanickam

It was the eve of my departure from India for the States, and I was preparing to take the train to Bombay. From there I was to sail. The lids of the trunks were clamped down, and the keys were being turned in the last locks. Someone said my presence was required in the living room, so I went in to find out who wanted me.

The living room was filled with women and girls. There were some men, too. The women were from my father's church and members of the Women's Union. I was met at the door by the president, who was followed by the others.

The president held in her hands a large brass tray filled with flowers — a garland of roses, tuberoses, the native *champak* and other flowers. There also were flowers that were not strung into a garland. The president put the garland round my neck, telling me its fragrance brought with it the good wishes of the Women's Union. Next she took one small flower and, saying a tiny prayer and blessing, placed it in my hair. She then held the tray while all the other mothers, one by one, did the same. My hair was still hanging down my back in a braid, and its whole length was soon covered with flowers of all colors and sizes.

When every mother had had her turn, the president, on behalf of the Union, bade me godspeed. This was followed by prayers offered by many in the group.

At last we sat down to my last meal at home. The food was served on large pieces of banana leaves, according to the Indian custom. On the table were plates heaped with purees and curried meat. It was a hurried meal, so there was nothing very elaborate. After this, there was *halva* for dessert.

INDIA

PUREE—bread substitute

Puree is an Indian substitute for bread.

2 cups flour	1½ heaping tablespoons butter
½ cup milk	¼ dessertspoon salt

Mix together, and add water to make a dough. The dough is of the right consistency when it does not stick to the fingers. This dough is then set aside for about two hours. (This makes for softness, but is not absolutely necessary.) The dough is then made into tiny balls, and rolled out thin. Fry in deep fat, one by one, till they puff out and turn slightly golden. Serve hot. Five portions.

CURRIED MEAT

1 pound meat	1 medium onion
1 dessertspoon (not heaped) cayenne pepper powder	½ dessertspoon turmeric
	½ dessertspoon allspice
1 dessertspoon (not heaped) curry powder	1 tablespoon raisins
	1 tablespoon shortening
1 dessertspoon vinegar	

The powders are all mixed together in a bowl with a spoonful of water. Set aside for a few minutes. The onion is sliced long and thin and fried in a tablespoon of shortening. When the onion is golden, the powder mixture is added and fried. The raisins are added now, and after stirring a few times, the meat (cut in small cubes) is added. When meat and spices are well mixed by stirring, the vessel is covered, and the meat cooks in its own juice, till the juice is almost all gone. Then enough water is added to cook the meat and to allow enough for gravy. Salt is added to taste. When the meat is well cooked, a dessertspoon of vinegar is stirred into the meat, and the dish is ready to serve five people.

Serve purees and fried meat with cooked vegetables, salads and pickels.

HALVA—dessert

2 cups cream of wheat	2 tablespoons butter and
2 tablespoons raisins	Crisco
1½ tablespoons cashew nuts	1 cup milk
¾ cup sugar	1½ cups water
¼ dessertspoon salt	1 cardamom pod, powdered

The cream of wheat is first roasted in a frying pan till slightly brown. Set aside. The nuts and raisins are then fried till golden in the butter and Crisco. The milk and water are then added. When this comes to a boil, the wheat is added and stirred well, till the water is almost all gone. Sugar and salt are then added. The mixture is stirred well till the *halva* does not stick to the spoon. The cardamom is then stirred into it, and the *halva* is ready. Before adding the milk and water, some of the fried nuts and raisins (1 tablespoon) may be taken out and used for decorating the top of the *halva* before serving.

Bread of Life

By MARY RAJAN

Late one afternoon an Indian Christian called on a missionary, Mr. Brown, to arrange for an interview for a Hindu friend of his. The missionary not only fixed the time for the interview but suggested that he bring his Hindu friend, Sunderam, for supper the next day if possible.

Mr. Sunderam accepted the invitation. He had been longing to talk with the missionary, Mr. Brown. However, he was taken aback by the fact that he was to eat with a Christian, and that, too, with a missionary.

The next day a very lovely Indian dinner was prepared, and Sunderam arrived with his Christian friend, on time. Sunderam did not talk much at the beginning. He was very quiet. But the friendliness shown by Mr. and Mrs. Brown and their children and the congenial atmosphere at the table and the pleasant conversation put Sunderam very much at ease, and most of the reservation and doubts on his part broke down even while they were eating. Needless to say he enjoyed his meal very much.

After dinner, Mr. Brown and Sunderam retired to the living room where they immediately began to talk on important things. Sunderam had been restless for months and had been going from one source to another, one friend to another, in search of the Truth — for something that would satisfy the deepest longing of his heart and soul. In short, he was seeking for the true God. Unfortunately, in his search for the Truth he was led to many people who were the wrong kinds of signposts, who instead of being a help to him led him farther away from God. So, even at this interview with Mr. Brown, he had misapprehensions. Still he was determined to seek for the Truth till he found it.

Sunderam had been a gangster. But the more he got in trouble with the authorities and with his family, the more he longed in some way to have the power to lead a changed life. He went to the temple regularly and prayed earnestly that he might be delivered from his sins, be given new power to live a different life, but to no avail. So it was with great eagerness and earnestness that he had come to Mr. Brown, hoping to be led to Truth and Peace.

Sunderam felt very much at home after the lovely dinner, and so, without wasting much time, he began to pour out his heart. He told of his failures, sins and crimes and how he longed for someone to deliver him from these chains and give him peace and joy. While listening closely to everything Sunderam was saying, Mr. Brown was very much in prayer, for he knew quite well that no man is saved by the power or the wisdom of human words but only by the power of God. He also knew that Sunderam was in earnest and, if some change did not come to him that night, he was planning to put an end to his life soon.

Mr. Brown began in very simple language to tell the story of Christ's life and death and how He could pardon sin and give power over it. Sunderam was very skeptical, as a simple story like this was not profound enough for his philosophical mind. He found the story of Salvation too simple, and he was building up a wall in his mind and heart against accepting this simple truth. He had come expecting some great teaching from an educated Western missionary.

Sunderam rose up to say good-by and go. Mr. Brown was confounded and was in real agony of soul. He did not know what else he could do to help that sinful, educated, cultured Hindu. However, guided by the spirit of God, he asked Sunderam if he minded having a word of prayer before they parted. Sunderam did not like this idea, but his mother had taught him always to be obliging and polite to his host. So out

56

of courtesy he complied, and they knelt down to pray. As Mr. Brown prayed, something miraculous happened.

The walls of prejudice, pride and doubt began to vanish from Sunderam's heart and mind, and instead, he broke down like a child and wept. For the first time in his life he prayed, "Lord Jesus have mercy on me and forgive me." He was on his knees for three hours weeping and praying, and he might have been seeing all of his past life as if on a cinema screen. When he got up from his knees, he was already a changed man. Christ had come into his life and had given him a new life. He felt that his most besetting habits left him all of a sudden, and he felt a new freedom, release, joy and peace.

Sunderam was not able to understand or explain this change that had come over him, but he knew that something had happened to him. At first he thought that Mr. Brown had performed some miracle over him, and he felt so good that he took out his purse to pay Mr. Brown. Mr. Brown explained to him that it was God's salvation coming to him and that it was free to all. But he asked Sunderam to be a witness for Christ.

Mrs. Brown and his Christian friend rejoiced with him when they were told. They sat and talked till the early hours of the morning. Sunderam was given advice as to what he should do next.

From that day onwards, he started to study the Bible and later on accepted baptism. In spite of being disowned and persecuted by his own family and friends, he has remained true to Christ and has been a witness who leads many others to Christ.

INDIA

MENU

Lime Rice or Plain Rice

Mutton *Kurma* or Meat Curry   Curds *Pachadi*

Payasam (dessert)

"Meat curry" may be substituted for "mutton *kurma*" as it is easier to prepare. But on special occasions when this particular meal is given, "mutton *kurma*" is the ideal thing.

LIME RICE

1 cup rice	3 tablespoons Crisco or oil
3 cups water	¼ teaspoon dry mustard seeds
2½ teaspoons salt	4 dry red chillies
4 limes or lemons	½ teaspoon fenugreek seeds
⅛ teaspoon turmeric powder	if available

Boil water. Add the salt. When water is boiling, add the rice. When the rice is almost cooked, extract the lemon or lime juice and mix it well with the rice. When the rice is well cooked, and the water evaporated, remove it from the fire. Heat the Crisco, add the mustard seeds. When they break open, add the fenugreek seeds and the turmeric and remove from fire. Add the cooked rice to the seasoning and mix well.

MUTTON KURMA

½ pound mutton	1 cup curds or yogurt
2 potatoes	1 cup coconut milk

1 teaspoon coriander leaves or mint leaves

PASTE	SEASONING
1 teaspoon coriander powder	2 tablespoons melted butter
1 teaspoon cumin powder	3 cloves
3 small pods garlic, finely grated	3 cardamom
1 inch cube fresh green ginger, grated	3 small cinnamon sticks
½ or 1 onion, grated	1 onion
½ teaspoon salt	
1 green chili, grated, or	
½ teaspoon chili powder	
¼ teaspoon turmeric powder	

Boil whole potatoes and cut them into cubes when cooked. Make the paste with the above ingredients, and mix it in the curds, and add them to the fresh meat. Heat the ghee, and fry whole cloves, cardamom, cinnamon sticks and chopped onion. Add the meat mixed with the paste and curds, and fry for about two minutes. Add water and boil till meat is cooked. Add cooked potatoes and coriander or mint leaves. Mash two or three cubes of cooked potatoes. Add coconut milk and let simmer.

COCONUT MILK: Grate one-half coconut. Add a little hot water, and squeeze the white milk from the coconut several times, until the grated coconut has no more white milk when pressed.

MEAT CURRY

1 pound meat—cut up	2 or 3 flakes of crushed garlic
1 onion—chopped	1 teaspoon grated fresh ginger
¼ teaspoon turmeric	
1 teaspoon coriander powder	
½ teaspoon red chili powder	2—3 tablespoons ghee or Crisco

1 or 2 tablespoons tomato paste or sour cream

Fry chopped onions till nearly brown in the ghee or Crisco. Add turmeric, red chili and coriander powder, ginger and garlic, mixed with a little water, to onions. Fry on slow fire till the ghee comes up. Add meat and fry. When meat gets brown, add hot water and salt. Potatoes may be added when the meat is half-cooked. After meat is cooked, add sour cream or tomato paste.

CURDS PACHADI

1 cup curds or yogurt	½ onion
1 ripe tomato	Salt to taste

Cut tomato and onion into very fine pieces (almost like grating), and add them to curds. Add salt. (Fresh grated ginger and green chili may be added if desired.)

PAYASAM—dessert

½ cup thinnest noodles	⅛ cup raisins
1 cup evaporated milk (or more)	2 tablespoons melted butter
5 almonds, chopped	Sugar as needed

½ teaspoon cardamom powder or 1 teaspoon or more vanilla
Water enough to cook noodles

Remove almond skins before chopping fine. Melt butter and fry almonds till golden brown. Remove almonds and fry raisins till they puff up. Remove them also. Break noodles into tiny bits. Fry in butter till some of them turn slightly brown. Add water, and cook. When noodles are almost cooked, add milk and sugar, and cook. Add the cardamom powder or vanilla, fried almonds and raisins. Remove from fire. Chill and serve with cookies or cake.

Jungle Picnic

By Miriam Robinson

Recently our girls had a picnic which deserves mention. The Junior Christian Endeavor gave a picnic in honor of those who had left their group to go into the High School group. We decided to go to a place about a mile from Golaghat. It was beneath a big tree, an open space with jungle on one side and a tea plantation about half a mile away on the other side. The girls had to carry everything there, including the water for the tea and the firewood. Games, singing and eating were enjoyed by all. We ate *lucies* and *tocurry*, spiced tea and fried peanuts.

INDIA

LUCIES—wafers

3 cups flour   ¼ cup shortening

Mix the flour and shortening together in the same manner that biscuits are mixed. Then add enough water so that they are the right consistency to roll very thin. The dough should be mixed well with the fingers. Make balls of the dough about 1½ inches in diameter. Then roll out each ball very thin and fry in deep fat. Serve with curried vegetables. Six portions.

TOCURRY—curried vegetables

2 cups potatoes, cubed   ½ cup water
1 large onion   2 cups carrots or pumpkin
2 teaspoons curry powder   Salt to taste

Slice onion thin. Drop into hot grease in a frying pan. When brown, add curry powder and water. When this mixture is boiling, add vegetables and salt and boil about an hour, stir once or twice. Drain before serving.

SPICED TEA

12 teacups water   1 bay leaf
   Tea leaves   5 or 6 pieces of cinnamon
   Milk and sugar for 12 cups   bark
      tea   6 whole cloves

Tea is made in Indian style like this: Bring the water to a boil. For a picnic, put tea leaves in a cloth bag and put in the boiling water; leave the tea leaves in the water until a dark amber color. When the tea bag is removed, the spices are added and also milk and sugar. Indian tea is always fixed with sugar and milk beforehand. After the tea has boiled with the spices, milk and sugar, then serve.

61

A Green Bluebeard

By RUTH THURMOND

Just after I had completed one year of language study I began my first assignment as a new and very green missionary in the A. B. M. Girls' High School in Nellore. The Indian women teachers decided they would give a *poolav* feast in honor of their new missionary.

So the common room of the Teachers' Home was cleaned and decorated, the food for the feast carefully prepared, the leaf plates spread in front of rows of mats. It was a hot day, as usual, but the place looked charming.

Miss Olive Jones and I were greeted warmly by the teachers, but they felt a bit shy about the new arrival. We sat down on the mats with the Indian women, except those who were serving the food. After the blessing was asked, Alice Veeraswamy thoughtfully handed each of us a gaily colored paper napkin with elephants printed in the corners. Mine was blue — my favorite color.

A big pile of fragrant rice *poolav* was heaped on each leaf plate, followed by various highly seasoned curries and savories. I was but a green missionary enjoying the delicious flavor of the food, perspiring profusely from the combined heat of the weather and the highly spiced food. Daintily I wiped my mouth again and again with my napkin. I looked up to see amused smiles on the faces of various teachers. What social blunder was I unconsciously committing? Finally, Alice Veeraswamy could contain her laughter no longer. She got up, found a mirror and asked me to look at myself.

One glance in the mirror was enough to convince me that I was no longer a green missionary, but rather a sure-enough bluebeard. The lovely blue napkin, wiped over my moist face, had turned it a rich blue.

We all laughed together. No longer was there a social wall between us. We were no longer strangers.

INDIA

RICE POOLAV

Rice *Poolav* is the favorite meal for a feast among our Telugu folks. Birthday and wedding feasts or other special celebrations are observed by inviting in friends to partake of a *poolav* meal. Soon after arrival, all guests wash their hands, then sit in rows on mats on the floor. Then they are served on leaf plates (made of banyan tree leaves stitched together or of a big plantain leaf). The main dish is *poolav;* other extras may be a *dahl* curry or curds with green chillies and onions added. For dessert, either fruit or a sweet dish like *Halva* may be served.

1 measure *poolav* rice or raw rice	½ coconut
3 quarts mutton	4 tablespoons salt
10 ounces *ghee* (butter or shortening)	8 bunches coriander leaves
	1/16 quart coriander seeds
10 ounces onions	1 bunch mint leaves
2½ ounces garlic	4 large tomatoes
2½ ounces green ginger	½ pint curds
Cloves, cinnamon and cardamom, *birinji* leaf	2½ ounces almonds
	½ pint cow's milk
2½ ounces green chillies	2 ounces *kum-kum-poo**

Ingredients to grind separately: coriander seeds, coconut, garlic, ginger, half cardamoms, cloves and cinnamon together, almonds.

To make *Kurma*: Place *Deksha* (pot with spout) on fire, add *ghee*, fry half cut onions, add unground cardamom, cloves and cinnamon, and *birinji* leaves, then the rest of the onions; after it is red, add the following ground stuffs: garlic, ginger, coriander seeds and coconut, fry lightly. Add coriander leaves, cut chillies, meat. Fry well. Add curds. Dissolve 4 fingers of salt in ½ pint of water and add with cut tomatoes. Cover. When the meat is three-fourths boiled, add ground coconut. Boil separately ½ pint of cow's milk until it is reduced to ¼ pint. Mix almonds and *kum-kum-poo*; add to mixture. Cook the rice until three-fourths boiled. Mix the rice in the *kurma*; add mint leaves. Remove bottom fire. Tie up the mouth of the *Deksha* with a white cloth and cover with a lid with live coals on. Stir and remove when rice looks dry.

* Unidentified.

Kuji

JAPAN

TOKYO

INLAND SEA

A Scrap of Paper

By Thomasine Allen

At five o'clock in the morning six policemen came to intern me. Naturally I had some difficulty in dressing as the men came popping in and out all the time to see that I did not hide any secret data. In one moment when they were out of the room I destroyed some private letters and was just on the verge of putting one little piece of paper in the stove when a man barged in and caught me. He told me not to destroy anything.

I was taken to the police station, and four of the men remained to search my house thoroughly. A long time afterwards I found out that, after a very careful searching, the only thing they took away with them was the little paper I was about to burn — for that seemed, in their eyes, exceedingly important. It was the recipe for a one-egg cake!

JAPAN

ONE-EGG CAKE

1 tablespoon butter	½ cup milk
1 cup sugar	1½ teaspoons baking powder
1 egg	1½ cups flour

A Party Dish

By FLORA ERNST

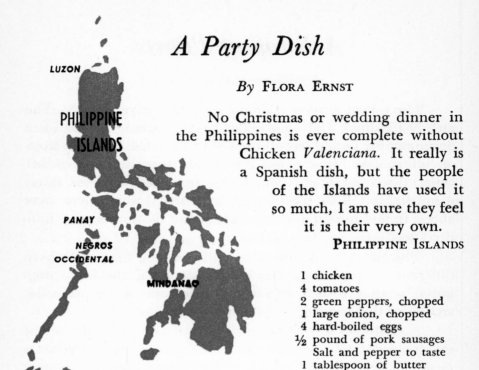

No Christmas or wedding dinner in the Philippines is ever complete without Chicken *Valenciana*. It really is a Spanish dish, but the people of the Islands have used it so much, I am sure they feel it is their very own.

PHILIPPINE ISLANDS

1 chicken
4 tomatoes
2 green peppers, chopped
1 large onion, chopped
4 hard-boiled eggs
½ pound of pork sausages
Salt and pepper to taste
1 tablespoon of butter
1 pound of rice

Cut the chicken into individual servings. Brown in pan with sausages. Add one cup of water and cook until tender. Cook onions in butter for five minutes, then add green peppers and cook for a few minutes more, then add tomatoes and cook for ten minutes. Add to chicken. Wash a pound of rice. Add; cook all together for twenty minutes or until rice is done. It should look rather dry in appearance. Serve on a platter and decorate with sliced hard-boiled eggs.

A Dormitory Party

By Elena Maquiso

The school year was almost over in the year 1948. The girls of Channon Hall decided to have a party. The Hall is a dormitory for girls who are enrolled in the College of Theology of Silliman University, but it has taken in girls from other colleges, too. Each girl invited another girl, and about thirty members of the faculty also were invited. Since there were about forty-three girls, there were a few more than one hundred people in the party that night.

The girls were divided into eight groups. They came from different sections of the Philippines. It was decided that each group would prepare a dish that was common in one particular section of the country.

Each group had a chairman who handed in a list of the things needed for the dish. The cook of the dormitory had a *tartanilla* (horse-drawn vehicle) full of things which she bought in the market.

Each group did its best and the whole day was full of activity and excitement. The party was a successful one and it was one Channon Hall experience that the girls will long remember.

The dish of the following recipe was prepared by a group of girls who came from one province. I selected this dish because it is the only one that I remember of the eight that were prepared. The girls of the group prepared too much and so the girls in the dormitory had to have the same soup for two days after the party!

PHILIPPINE ISLANDS

PANSIT MOLO—pastry in soup

PASTRY

1 cup flour	¼ teaspoon salt
3 egg yolks	¼ cup water

Sift flour and salt. Add egg yolks and knead with the fingers. Add water and work until the dough is smooth and fine. Roll to a thin sheet on a board. Cut into small triangular pieces.

FILLING

1 cup ground pork	2 tablespoons chopped *kutsay*
5 tablespoons *toyo*	Pinch of pepper
2 egg yolks	

Mix these ingredients and wrap in the triangular pieces of pastry, pressing the sides to seal them together.

SOUP

1 chicken, small pieces	5 cups shrimp soup
1½ cups sliced shrimp	10 cups chicken soup
8 teaspoons chopped garlic	½ cup chopped *kutsay*
8 teaspoons *toyo*	Salt

Fry garlic, onion, shrimp. Add chicken and fry about eight minutes. Add *toyo* and cook some more. Add shrimp and chicken soup and boil slowly for one hour.

When ready to serve, drop wrapped mixture in the soup and boil for five minutes.

EUROPE

Doughnuts
for
Fellowship

By LEXIE FERRELL CRAIG

This recipe for doughnuts is one which I have just received from Sister Else who still works for the refugee boys at a home in Hanover, Germany. These doughnuts were prepared by her on the final night of our work project there late in August, 1949.

This story was told by Hans Arndt as he gave our closing devotions that night. There were at the party twenty-three boys who had escaped from the Russian Zone and twelve Americans.

BLEST BE THE TIE THAT BINDS OUR HEARTS

It was August, 1939. Ronald Bell had come over to Germany with twenty-five young British Baptists. I joined this group with fifteen German boys and girls. We had a wonderful time. Traveling up the Rhine from Cologne we found ourselves finally in the Black Forest in a settlement of the Moravian-Brethren called Keenigsfeld. The fellowship became a very real one. After a week the political situation changed suddenly. A telegram came from London.

"Wish you a speedy and safe return." We called up the British ambassador in Frankfurt that night. We listened to the British broadcasting.

The next morning came. A happy group gathered at the breakfast table. After the breakfast I had to give the announcement asking everybody to be prepared to leave this place in thirty minutes. No one of us will ever forget the following moment. We read the Bible, prayed together, joined hands and sang "Blest be the tie that binds our hearts." Looking into the faces of those fine young people who, after the days of fellowship, had to realize the fact that perhaps in a short time they would meet again fighting one another on the battlefield, I felt definitely: There is something wrong in this world.

I brought the British friends to the border. There was the train. Ronald Bell stood outside on the platform. We said, "Good-by." He was the last English Baptist who stood on German ground before the war. In 1946 I was the first German Baptist to come to England. There was no question: we were still friends because we were brethren in Christ.

GERMANY

DOUGHNUTS

1,000 grams flour	1 egg
20 grams shortening	Pinch of salt
20 grams fresh yeast	½ to 1 pint of milk
60 grams sugar	Fat for baking (lard or shortening)

Stir the yeast with half a cup of warm milk until smooth. Put the yeast into the middle of flour and put the dish with flour and yeast in a warm place for about ten minutes. After that time, mix all other ingredients with flour and yeast. Add milk to get a dough you can roll out, later on. First, keep the dough in a warm place about another hour, until the dough rises. Now roll out the dough and form little round pieces which have to rise again at least half an hour. Then put the pieces into a pan of boiling fat and leave them in until they are brown. Turn the warm doughnuts in sugar.

Good success and good appetite!

—SISTER ELSE
Germany

71

Gisela's Black Snail

By HERBERT MASCHER

The whole story began when Gisela had to do some shopping for her mother before going to school. She bought freshly baked bread and noodles. My, what a wonderful aroma the bread had! It peeped out of the bag very temptingly, and, before she knew it, Gisela had broken off the end and put it into her mouth. However, in the process of breaking off the end of the bread, the paper bag tore, and noodles scattered over the path before the garden gate.

Oh, oh, if only no one notices, thought Gisela. I'll quickly put the noodles back into the bag. I'll just brush off the dust a bit, and, though they look a bit gray, that could be the color of the flour. But crawling over the noodles was a fat, black horse-snail. Dare I take the noodles from the ground? Oh, yes, into the bag they must all go, otherwise the bag will not be full. But no one must see!

"Here are the noodles, Mother," said Gisela, "and I have put the bread in the bread box." It was darker in the cupboard where the bread box was kept. No one would notice that the end crust was gone.

"That's fine, Gisela," her mother commended her. "When you come from school at noon, I shall have a nice plate of noodle soup for you."

Well, that went well, thought Gisela. No one saw — and no one would tell. Gisela wondered; was there perhaps someone who had seen her? She kept thinking of the noodles and of the horrible snail.

During German period in school Gisela's class read the story of "The King with the Purple Cloak." The teacher, Miss Heine, told about the purple snail and said that some snails are poisonous. Poisonous snails, pondered Gisela!

"Are the poisonous snails fat and black?" she asked Miss Heine.

"Yes, yes, very fat and black," Miss Heine replied, impatient to continue the story and annoyed by the interruption.

Gisela heard nothing more. Now what would happen? The family were at home eating the noodle soup with the poisonous snail, and perhaps by the time she arrived home they would all be deathly ill. But it was only twelve noon, and the family would not have lunch so early; perhaps she could still save them! The clock had hardly struck twelve when Gisela ran out of the schoolroom, down the stairs and over the streets to her home, despite the fact that the morning session was not over until one o'clock.

Now everyone would find out what kind of a girl Gisela Klein was. Fraulein Heine would be asking for her, and tomorrow — unbearable to think of — what could she say when everyone knew what she had done. And all her schoolmates. How dreadful! And yet, was it so bad? If, through Gisela's fault, her mother and Hanna and Werner and Anneliese — no, no, she could not bear to think of it. It simply must not be!

She ran so fast she was out of breath.

There was the house, Number 23, and her family was eating noodle soup with poisonous snail sauce!

The street was so empty — the neighbors looked so peculiar — down the street there was an automobile — yes, it looked like an ambulance!

The hallway seemed deserted as Gisela entered the house, only two flies were buzzing about. Gisela slowed her pace. She stood before the kitchen door for two full minutes, and finally she turned the knob of the door.

There they all sat at the table — all well and happy — handing their mother their empty soup plates. Werner was at the stove, scraping the soup pot with meticulous care. Gisela's share had been set aside and was on the back of the stove in a small blue enamel pot.

All her fears were unwarranted; the soup had harmed none of them, and no one would know what had happened to the noodles.

Despite that fact, Gisela stammered, "Mother, I didn't know — the noodles — with the snail — yes, I did bite off the crust of the bread, and all the noodles fell on the ground — right there where a fat snail was crawling — I didn't want anyone to know what I had done and so I quickly picked up the noodles and put them back into the bag — and it was so terrible — please, Mother, please, forgive me!"

Werner said, "There stands the snail princess!" Hanna and Anneliese said, "Brr!" and "Ugh!"

Mother scolded a little, but of course she forgave Gisela.

It was as if a stone had dropped from Gisela's heart.

She was so happy, she even offered to do the dishes, which really was a concession for Gisela.

Now when Gisela wishes to do something which she does not want anyone to see, she thinks of the noodles with the snail sauce — and she immediately changes her mind. I wonder why?

GERMANY

CHICKEN NOODLE SOUP

Frances A. Heine

1 four-pound chicken, cut in
   pieces
3 quarts cold water
1 onion, sliced

1 carrot, sliced
1 bay leaf
1 teaspoon parsley

Wash and clean chicken carefully. Cover with cold water. Add vegetables and seasoning and let simmer for three hours or until chicken is tender. Skim off fat. Remove chicken, strain soup. Bring again to boiling point and add two cups of noodles.

NOODLES: 2 eggs; ½ teaspoon salt; 1 cupful flour. Beat eggs, add salt and as much flour as can be worked into the eggs. Cover and let stand thirty minutes. Roll out thin and spread on cloth to dry for one hour. Roll up like jelly-roll and slice very thin. Spread out on a cloth ready for soup.

—NEW YORK

The Square Apple

By Herbert Mascher

Leonhard had a wonderful surprise for his friends! Their eyes grew very large as he showed them an apple which had the form of a building block. It was a real apple, with red and green skin and a fine aroma. But how could an apple grow square?

After the apple tree blossomed, Leonhard had taken a small square bottle and fastened it to the end of a twig on which there was a very small apple which fitted into the bottle. That was all that Leonhard did. The rest was done by the sun, the rain and the bottle.

The apple grew round like all the other apples, but when it reached the walls of the bottle, its form changed. The bottle gave the apple its form. Finally, the apple completely filled the square bottle.

With the other ripe apples, Leonhard picked the apple in the bottle from the tree and carefully broke the bottle. And what did he have? An apple with six sides and twelve corners like a building block!

People are like this square apple. When we grow, our environment, our parents, our teachers, our friends are influential in forming the right pattern for our lives. They try to influence us to take the form which God wills for us, according to the Apostle Paul, "Whatsoever things are true, whatsoever things are honorable, whatsoever things are just, whatsoever things are pure, whatsoever things are lovely, whatsoever things are of good report."

Thus we may grow to be good Christian men and women, following our perfect example, Christ Jesus. Then we shall remain in God's love and follow His word as we were taught to do. Without Him we can do nothing; therefore, we must trust Him and follow His Word.

GERMANY

Family Reunion

By ROSALIE OLSON

My brother and I had the joy and privilege of spending the summer of 1950 in Sweden. July ninth was one of the most delightful days of my life — a reunion of relatives on the farm where my father was born, and I also, in Moljesta. Naturally, we had an abundance of food, and the Christian fellowship was so inspiring!

There were twenty of us, and on a table in the living room was the first course, smorgasbord which included Swedish meat balls, cheeses and all the rest. Around the room were small coffee tables, where we sat after filling our plates. There was one course after the other, but no coffee for about two hours. Later we had that and dessert out in the garden. These recipes were just a part of this festivity. There were other foods that I would not know how to describe!

ILLINOIS

SAFFRON BREAD

Make a sponge of 1 quart flour, 2 cups warm water, 3 yeast cakes. Keep warm until light. Steep 25 cents worth of saffron, as for tea, strain, and add liquid to sponge. Mix 1 pound lard with a little butter; add 1 pound sugar, 1 pound raisins, 1 pound currants, ½ pound chipped citron, a little nutmeg. Work into sponge, and let rise. Form loaves, and let rise again until light. Bake in moderate oven one hour.

KOLDOLMAR—cabbage rolls

1 large head cabbage	1 pound pork hamburger
1 pound beef hamburger	2 cups cooked rice
Salt and pepper to taste	

Put the cabbage head in salted water for about 10 minutes; cut out inner hard stem. In a large kettle of boiling salted water, cook this cabbage until so soft, leaves bend. Mix beef, pork, salt and pepper and cooked rice. Put 1 heaping tablespoon of this mixture into each cabbage leaf. Fold carefully and wrap string around to keep it from breaking. Brown in butter; then remove to roaster, add some butter and a little water. Simmer 1 to 2 hours. Add more water to make enough gravy. Remove string and serve.

SWEDISH FRUIT SOUP

Cook ½ cup raisins, small stick of cinnamon, 1 cup prunes, pinch of salt. Then add 1 quart grape juice, and 3 tablespoons cornstarch, dissolved in cold water. Before chilling add a few slices of lemon.

SWEDISH RYE BREAD

Heat and let cool till lukewarm: 3 cups potato water, 1 tablespoon salt, 3 tablespoons brown sugar. Add 3½ cups rye flour and 1 cake compressed yeast, and let rise. Add 5 tablespoons molasses or 2 or 3 teaspoons melted shortening. Add white flour until hard enough to form into loaves.

STRAWBERRY DESSERT

Bake cake in a tube pan. Fill the center with whole strawberries. Pile whipped cream high over all the cake. Garnish generously with whole strawberries.

Sunday Supper

By Evelyn B. Bell

Some years ago a Zurich doctor inaugurated a health center, similar to the Battle Creek Sanatorium in the United States. He emphasized the importance of getting necessary vitamins through eating an abundance of fresh fruits and vegetables. Among the dishes served at his sanatorium daily was one which rapidly become very popular with the Zurichers and today is found on all the hotel and restaurant menus in this vicinity. The Swiss gave this dish the name of its famous creator, Dr. Bircher, and called it "Birchermuesli."

Whenever we have guests from other parts of the world, we like to serve this dish and are yet to find one "foreigner" who does not enjoy it. Since it is a meal in itself, it is especially good for Sunday evening supper served with cheese sticks and a hot drink.

BIRCHERMUESLI—fruit dessert

Take one cup of uncooked oatmeal (the quick kind). Add enough milk to make a thick paste. Let it stand awhile, then add from three to seven kinds of finely-chopped fruits, about three cups altogether. When *fraise de bois,* tiny wild strawberries, are in season, they add a delicious flavor. Bananas are always good. Mix in about a third of a cup of sweetened lemon juice and a half cup of ground nuts. Add salt, sugar or honey to taste, depending, of course, on the kinds of fruit used. Let it stand in the refrigerator until time to serve. Then fold in a cup or more of whipped cream. This will serve four persons. Your guests will ask for the recipe!

SWITZERLAND

THE AMERICAS –
LATIN
AMERICA

Abelardo's Birthday Party

By Jorgelina Lozada

One day Mother and I received an invitation for tea in the home of Abelardo. We were surprised, for Abelardo had been in kindergarten only a few weeks, and the family had not attended church services. Therefore we were not well acquainted with the family. But all this made us happy to accept the invitation.

Upon arriving we were courteously received into a humble home which was very clean and orderly. We soon learned that we were attending a birthday party for the little son. Just before we were served at the table the mother handed me the New Testament I had given Abelardo a short time before and said, "Please read from this book which I know you read often, and, if you will, do us the honor to ask God's blessing on our home. We are so happy and feel so honored to have you with us today."

Imagine my joy at being asked to read God's word in a home where the real Christ was not known as their Savior. What a marvelous opportunity to testify! When I had read and offered the prayer, to our surprise the mother brought in, not the customary birthday cake with candles but a platter heaped with *empanadas,* one of the favorite national dishes. Then we were served cocoa which is customary instead of coffee when it is a child's birthday. The mother smiled and said, "I made the *empanadas* instead of the cake because I know Miss Lozada likes them."

During that hour of comradeship with expressions of affection a very intimate relationship began to develop. The sequel to the story is beautiful: All the family have accepted Christ as their Savior and have become members of the church. This came to pass because of the friendship started in the kindergarten and the New Testament Abelardo received as a gift from his teacher.

ARGENTINA

EMPANADAS—spiced meat tarts

4 cups flour	2 tablespoons oleomargarine

8 to 12 tablespoons liquid—half milk, half water

Mix well and add liquid (half milk and half water) sufficient to make a dough which can be rolled to the thinness of pie dough. Then cut pieces the size and shape of a saucer.

3 cups of ground meat	2 eggs
Salt, pepper, cinnamon, cloves	A little finely chopped onion
	A few raisins and olives

Fry the onion first, add the chopped meat and then the other ingredients without allowing the mixture to become dry. Spread the mixture on half of the circle and also sprinkle with egg, two of which have been hard boiled and chopped up.

Close the half pie, dampened on the edges, pinch together and fry as you would doughnuts, in hot grease, until brown.

Upon removing the *empanadas* from the grease, sprinkle a bit of sugar over them.

Serve hot or cold for tea, picnic, garden party or at mealtime.

Havana

CUBA

Santiago

Emergencies
in the Santiago Church

By Sara Pais De Molina

Sunday school had just closed in the Baptist church in Santiago de Cuba, and the last churchgoers were on their way home, to return in the evening for the regular big service.

The minister was an old, rugged man, a widower. He lived next door to the church with his daughter and son-in-law and their five children. In an emergency he looked to his daughter for assistance.

"The Secretary and the architect from the Home Mission Society have just arrived in town and they telephoned from the hotel. I would like to bring them home for lunch. Do you think you can manage?"

Mrs. Molina caught her breath, then promised, "I'll try." Leaving her father to bring the guests, she went home to plan for last-minute changes without sending out for anything on Sunday. It was lucky they usually had a pretty big noon meal after Sunday school.

Let me see, she mused. Fruit cocktail; Americans like that, and they enjoy diced papaya and mango besides the more familiar fruit. Then steak, eggplant fritters, *congri* (the typical national dish of rice and beans), avocado salad, guava pie for dessert and coffee, Cuba's dark, thick coffee in small cups. The secretary had visited Cuba before and was familiar with it, but the architect would be glad to taste it for the first time.

While Mrs. Molina was helping her maid to set the table, Danny, the youngest child, rushed into the room.

"Mother!" He stopped short in his tracks, looked at the hand-embroidered tablecloth and grandmother's silver and groaned disgustedly. "Oh, no! Company again. I don't want to eat at the table."

"Nobody asked you, silly. Babies can eat in the kitchen. More elbow room for us. May I sit with the guests, Mother?" asked Paul, anxiously.

"Of course, there is room enough. How wonderful that you boys behave like angels when we have company. Those who know you think I am pretending when I say so."

Paul gave her a suspicious look. Did she know that the day before he and Frank had been passing French fried potatoes to each other under the table while their father was returning thanks? No, he had been sure her eyes were closed. But he wasn't very sure that that little telltale who sometimes spied on them from behind her latticed fingers hadn't been telling on them. But Mother's praise sounded sincere. Let sleeping dogs alone.

Danny was still whimpering: "I won't eat at the table, and I won't eat leftovers in the kitchen."

"You big baby," pacified his mother. "Nobody eats leftovers in the kitchen. Everybody is served from the platters. Ma Emily will give you your lunch first."

After a while, everything was ready, and the visitors arrived. They had been around town, looking at the damages caused by an earthquake a few weeks before. The eastern part of the island is geologically younger than the rest of the island; the settling process is not finished yet; and once in a while there are tremors, either isolated or in a series. It is no fun to hear that deep rumble, as if the earth were groaning, and to feel it shaking.

This time *Oriente* province had just gone through a rather severe quake. People were thrown from their beds at two o'clock in the morning, roofs and doors cracked and rattled, and brick walls toppled over like so many houses made of cards. The toll of lives had not been too severe, but there had been a score of casualties, many wounded and much loss of property. The Baptist church, an old building, was damaged on one side, so that one of the walls had to be demolished and a wooden one erected in its place until final steps could be taken for the new building so long wanted. That was the reason for the visit of the secretary and the architect.

During the dinner, conversation flowed about the usual topics: church work, social conditions, the earthquake, of course, and the possibilities for the new building. The American visitors enjoyed the Cuban dishes and said so. Finally, as they were leaving the table, the architect said:

"I certainly enjoyed the rice and beans, Mrs. Molina. Would you give me the recipe for my wife? I am sure she would like to cook it the Cuban way."

That took Mrs. Molina by surprise, but she promised to send a recipe to his New York office. She thought that there was nothing special about *congri* and her guest was merely being polite, so she soon forgot about it.

In a year or two, Mrs. Molina met the architect again, in New York, and he said: "I never got that rice and beans recipe, Mrs. Molina." She excused herself saying she could not imagine he really cared.

A few months later, the architect died, and another was sent by the mission board to erect a much-needed building for the Baptist Church in Santiago de Cuba, one of the largest in the island. Old-timers remember with gratitude Dr. G. Pitt Beers as the man used by the Lord to understand the problem, take it by the horns and find the right solution.

Here is the recipe. I'm sorry it wasn't forwarded before.

Cuba

CUBAN CONGRI—rice and beans

½ pound beans (black or red)
4 pints water
1 small green pepper
4 tablespoons oil
1 medium onion

2 medium-sized peppers
2 garlic cloves
1 teaspoon salt
1 pound rice
4 garlic cloves (unpeeled)

4 tablespoons lard or 2 ounces bacon

Soak beans overnight in measured water. Boil them in this water with the small pepper until soft. Fry slightly: oil, chopped onion, peppers and mashed peeled garlic cloves (2) until onion is golden colored. Add salt and leave on slow fire for 10 minutes more. Have rice previously washed. If the liquid in which the beans were cooked is less than 4 cups, add enough hot water to make the 4 cups. Cook on full burner until rice is boiling. Then lower heat until rice is cooked. When it begins to get dry, lower heat still more and let rice stay over very slow fire until grains are separated.

If you use the 4 tablespoons of lard, fry the unpeeled cloves until golden, strain lard and pour over rice and serve. If bacon is preferred, fry slightly and use the fat instead of the 4 tablespoons of lard. Arrange the strips of bacon on the platter.

A Baptismal Fete

By Ivah Heneise and Mae Kelly

The following Haitian dinner is the standard meal served, with variations, on "festive" occasions. This particular repast was served to the visiting pastors and missionaries by the host church at a baptismal "fete."

Baptisms in Haiti are accompanied by much rejoicing and feasting. Visitors come from neighboring churches, sometimes traveling a day or more to attend the baptism.

The baptisms are held in the rivers of Haiti, in Jordanlike simplicity. The Christians usually walk the one or two miles to the river, single file, singing hymns as they go. At the riverside, a service is held, and then the candidates are baptized. As the number of candidates sometimes exceeds three hundred, several pastors baptize together in the river.

These pastors are the honored guests of the host church and are served a banquet after the morning's activities. They sit together at a table, eating in western fashion with western utensils. The crowd that is served with them, however—the visitors from neighboring churches—does not fare quite so well. On the occasion when this meal was served, the pastors sat as usual at the table, while the others gathered in groups, six or eight around one large bowl of rice, beans and chicken. This bowl was passed back and forth, each guest taking a bite in turn and all using the one large spoon provided with each bowl.

HAITI

86

HAITIAN DINNER

Fruit cocktail (pineapple, oranges, grapefruit, bananas, papayas)

Green beans with Creole Sauce

Chicken and Macaroni

Banana and boiled plantain (ripe bananas cut lengthwise, fried quickly)

Rice and beans

Pain Patate (sweet potato bread or cake)

Coffee, black and sweet

CREOLE SAUCE

Fry an "arbitrary" amount of onions, garlic, thyme and scallions in a small amount of fat. Add chopped tomatoes and ripe sweet peppers (or green), season with salt and pepper, add flour and water. (Tomato sauce may be added.)

CHICKEN AND MACARONI

Cut chicken in serving pieces. Dip in seasoned flour, brown in skillet. Add chopped onions and tomatoes, fry. Add flour and water (almost cover). Simmer half an hour (or until sauce thickens slightly). Add macaroni (already boiled) and simmer in sauce fifteen minutes to a half hour more.

RICE AND BEANS

RICE: Rice should be brown, unpolished. One tablespoon of oil for each cup of rice should be mixed with the dry rice. Seasoning added: minced onions and garlic, or their juice. Three cups of water to a cup of rice are then added. Cook rice slowly until the water is gone and the grains are separate.

BEAN SAUCE—*Sauce Pois:* Presoak red kidney beans, then boil until tender (4 cups water to 1 cup beans). Put through a large-holed sieve or food grinder. Add thyme, scallion, chopped onions, salt and pepper to taste. Finally, add 2 cups of water for each cup of pureed beans. Boil until mixture thickens. Some beans are always kept whole (not pureed) to add at the end to enhance the appearance. Pour over rice and serve.

PAIN PATATE

Grate 5 raw sweet potatoes (medium-sized). Add one grated coconut (moist, shredded coconut may be substituted).

Add ½ cup sugar, 1 teaspoon ground cinnamon, ½ teaspoon ground nutmeg, ¼ teaspoon ground cloves. Add 4 tablespoons oil or melted butter and 1 cup milk. Mix well. Pour in greased baking dish, dot with butter, bake slowly until cake is done. A knife inserted will be dry on removal.

HAITIAN CREOLE DINNER MENU

IVAH HENEISE

Goat ragout with *ti-cocomb* and avocado

Roasted breadfruit slices

Crushed *mirliton* with tomatoes and shallots

Plantain, ripe—baked; and green—fried chips

Rice and red bean sauce

Salad of water cress, calabash, and green onions

French dressing—Vinegar and oil

Cassava bread

Pain patate (sweet potato pudding)

Coffee

SOME NOTES ON PROCEDURES

The ragout can be made of beef, browned, stewed in a sauce of water, flour, tomatoes, sage, salt and lots of pepper. A little garlic and onions are usually added, too. The *ti-cocomb* can be replaced by cucumber, skin and all, cut up and cooked with the meat. A few avocado slices dropped in at the last moment contribute to the flavor. The *mirliton* may be replaced by any kind of squash, mashed, and cooked again with onions and tomatoes cut up in it. Bananas may be substituted for plantain if necessary. The rice may be cooked plain, and the sauce poured over it.

In making the sauce, the red beans are soaked overnight, seasoned well and cooked a long time, after which they are either crushed with a potato masher or put through a large-holed sieve. They should have plenty of juice. There is no substitute for cassava. The *pain patate* is made of grated sweet potatoes, grated fresh coconut, the milk and water of this coconut, eggs, sugar, lots of cinnamon and nutmeg. If fresh coconut is not available, regular shredded coconut may be used and milk added.

POTATO PONE

ALICE M. WOOD

1 pound sweet potatoes	1 cup brown sugar
1 coconut in shell	¼ teaspoon salt
½ teaspoon grated nutmeg	

Grate the sweet potatoes and coconut separately. Pour onto coconut 1½ cups of water. Squeeze through fine colander. Sweeten this coconut milk with the cup of sugar. Add salt and nutmeg. Stir all this into grated potato. Cook over fire until thickened. Pour into baking dish. Bake until mixture sets. Raisins may be added if desired.

HAITI

A Stretching Party

By ELLA H. KEPPLE

Until I helped the women of Cosio, a small rural locality in Central Mexico, make *Buñuelos* for a New Year's party, I never really realized what a social occasion the making of them could be. Early in the morning, one of the women made up the dough and put it to rise. Then in the afternoon, we met in her home to "stretch" the *buñuelos* so that they could dry and be ready to fry in the evening.

The "stretching" was not done in the kitchen as one would suppose, but in the front room of the house. Each woman sat in a low chair; if she had small children they were on the floor beside her; if they slept, she folded her *rebozo* or shawl under them. A snow-white napkin or doily, embroidered and edged with crocheted lace, nicely starched and ironed, was placed on her knee. Then she took a ball of the dough, worked it a minute in her hands, and then began to stretch it on the napkin. She stretched it carefully and patiently until it was almost as large as a dinner plate and nearly paper thin, all the while participat-

89

ing with animation in the gossip that was exchanged. The stretched *buñuelos* were spread on clean sheets on beds and tables to dry. When the men and boys came to the party, they were fried in pottery bowls of deep fat. They were served hot with cinnamon tea and were delicious.

MEXICO

BUNUELOS—fritters

4 cups flour	1 teaspoon ground cinnamon
2 teaspoons baking powder	2 tablespoons lard
1 teaspoon salt	2 eggs, well beaten
½ cup sugar	Enough water to make a good dough

Sift dry ingredients into a large bowl. Work in lard, eggs, water. Make the dough and put aside for several hours, if possible. Cut the dough into pieces the size of walnuts; on a floured dough-board roll them out till they are the size of saucers and as thin as possible. Let dry for at least half an hour. Fry in deep fat. Sprinkle with sugar. Serve hot or cold.

CINNAMON TEA

These are good with cinnamon tea which is made by adding cinnamon to boiling water and allowing to simmer a few minutes. Let stand to redden. Sweeten to taste, adding sugar or lemon if desired

In Time of Celebration

By Ella H. Kepple

When I was about to be married twenty years ago, the alumnae of Alpha chapter of Pi Zeta Kappa gave me a recipe box, and each girl put into it her favorite recipe. I shall always be thankful to Agatha Thornton for the Chocolate Cake recipe which has been my "ever present help in time of celebrations." It makes a big, luscious cake and really never fails. In two of our mission dormitories it has helped celebrate many a birthday, saint's day or other event of note.

Once the boys in the dormitory were having a holiday from school. I offered to let them cook dinner, anything they wanted within reason. They had fried rabbit from our warren, peas from our garden, their usual beans and tortillas, and chocolate cake made by this recipe.

I stood by while they mixed the cake, and I heated the oven for them. Then I was called away. When I returned, they had the cake batter in a kettle on a hot charcoal fire, cooking it like a pudding with much careful stirring. I had them transfer it to cake pans in a hurry and pop it into the oven. Strange as it may seem, it turned out well, a bit chewy perhaps, but ever so good. There never was a prouder bunch of boys!

MEXICO

NEVER-FAIL CHOCOLATE CAKE

1½ cups sugar	½ teaspoon salt
½ cup shortening	½ cup cocoa
3 tablespoons boiling water	2 cups flour
1½ cups milk	2 eggs
2 teaspoons vanilla	1 teaspoon soda

Put ½ cup sugar into a small saucepan, add cocoa and 1 cup of milk. Stir until it boils five minutes. Remove from fire, add vanilla and let cool. Beat sugar and shortening to a cream, add eggs and beat two minutes. Now add remainder of milk, soda dissolved in boiling water, flour, salt and chocolate mixture. Mix carefully and put into two large, greased and floured cake tins. Bake in a moderate oven 25 minutes. Put together with seven minute or fudge icing.

Without Money

By Daniel Lopez De Lara

When I was just beginning to become interested in the Gospel, I was a delegate from the young peoples' group of the Christian church of San Luis Potosí to a convention of the Churches of Christ, in a ranch town, Cipress and San Antonio de Pánuco, State of Zacatecas.

In the home where I stayed, during a conversation, I remarked that it was very easy to prepare delicious dishes, using what could be produced in the country, without spending any money. After hearing this, one of the daughters of the house immediately asked me, "Do you know how to prepare any?"

Not wishing to appear ignorant in the art of cooking and especially after having said what I had, I replied with assurance, "Yes, indeed!"

"Very well," she answered, with a twinkle in her eye. "Then tomorrow you are going to show us how to make such a dish, for we want to learn how!"

I couldn't sleep for thinking of my commitment. Fortunately I remembered a recipe for stuffed chicken. The following day I asked for the ingredients, and up to this day everybody in that house remembers that the stuffed chicken was very good.

To crown my culinary accomplishment, I proposed that the next day we make "parched corn in syrup."

Mexico

STUFFED CHICKEN

The chicken is dressed and well cleaned. Chop fine a little onion and garlic, dice potatoes, carrots and Mexican sausage. Mix; add peas and season with salt and pepper. Stuff the chicken. Cook in an oven until tender. When tender, the chicken is served with a hot pepper sauce: Toast tomatoes and green peppers on fire until skins may be removed, peel, salt, grind fine.

PARCHED CORN IN SYRUP

Make a thick syrup with three pounds of dark brown sugar (one kilo and a half). When a little makes a soft ball in water, add the parched corn to the syrup, stirring constantly to avoid sticking. Then, with the hands moistened in water, make the corn into small balls, working very rapidly. This candy is very much liked by the country children.

Does It Bite?

By Mabel V. Young

We were invited to the home of one of our pupils who lived in a village not far from Puebla. For the festive occasion the family had prepared *mole,* which was the main dish and practically the only one, though accompanied with *tortillas* aplenty.

Before beginning to eat the *mole,* I asked "*¿Pica* (Does it bite)?" and was told, no, that it was not hot (with pepper). Accordingly I took an ordinary mouthful, but before I could swallow it, the tears were running down my cheeks, as the festive food burned its way down my throat.

"*Pobrecita* (poor thing)," said the friends. "It does not bite us."

Now I always try a tiny, tiny bit of the mixture to decide what to do next.

Mexico

MOLE POBLANO—Mexican chili

¼ pound each of *chiles*—dark; flat; *chipocle*
¼ pound sesame seeds
¼ pound raisins
¼ pound peanuts and almonds
2 *tortillas* well toasted
50 grams cinnamon

3 plantains with skin (cooking bananas)
2 cakes of chocolate
1 piece of garlic
1 teaspoon annis
6 ground cherries
2 large tomatoes

Brown the *chiles* and sesame seed. Later take out veins of the *chiles.* Fry each of these separately: *chipocle,* almonds, peanuts, the plantain sliced with skin on, ground cherries and tomatoes. Then grind ingredients until they form a paste, without water. Fry the raisins, garlic, annis, cinnamon and add to paste. Grind chocolate and *tortillas,* without frying: add to paste. Heat a little lard in a large pan and fry the paste slightly. Add this to meat and broth of pork or turkey or chicken. Cook together until tender. It looks like chocolate gravy with grease on the surface and pieces of meat within. Watch out, it bites! But it is good!

Watermelon Fresco

By Phebe Pixley

Mrs. Nicholson, the American Minister's wife introduced Watermelon *Fresco* to us when we called on her about work in the Foreign Women's Society. Later, our Baptist missionary group of ten, and seven Central American missionaries, had Thanksgiving dinner together. We served small glasses of ice cold watermelon juice, with lime juice to taste, as an appetizer. Everyone seemed to enjoy it immensely.

Nicaragua

FRESCO—watermelon punch

Press watermelon through a colander. Chill the extract. Add lime or lemon juice to taste.

Potatoes!

By Genoveva Rios de Bahamonde

From an actual conversation:

Host: It makes me a bit homesick to serve this dish; it is one of my mother's favorites.

Guest: These potatoes are delicious; it is sometimes hard to get good potatoes. I prefer Maine potatoes.

Guest: Idaho potatoes were what we had at home.

Guest: Irish potatoes are the best. (Everyone turns toward our Irish guest, who blushes slightly.)

Host: Why are they called Irish potatoes? It is strange.

Irish Guest: They were brought from Ireland to America.

Host: And who gave Ireland her potatoes?

Irish Guest: I don't know. Sir Walter Raleigh, I guess. He got them from somewhere in the New World.

Host: From Peru, my homeland. The Spaniards took them to Spain and from there they went to France, England and Ireland.

You have heard of the Inca Empire? It had a population of about ten million people, raised on potatoes among other foods. The greatest contribution Peru made to humanity was not the gold or precious metals from her mines, but potatoes — grown today all over the world.

PERU

HUANCAINA (Wankaeenah) POTATOES

6 medium-sized potatoes
½ pound cottage cheese
⅓ cup olive oil
1 tablespoon lemon juice
½ teaspoon minced garlic
1 teaspoon minced onion

¼ teaspoon ground red peppers
1 tablespoon minced parsley
Salt to taste
Yellow vegetable coloring
3 hard boiled eggs

Boil potatoes, peel and mash while warm. Add salt to taste and shape into balls; arrange on a flat dish. Sauté garlic, onion and red pepper with 2 tablespoons olive oil over low fire. Stir constantly until very lightly browned. In a bowl, mix cottage cheese with this, add lemon juice, salt to taste, and coloring (2 or 3 drops). Beat with spoon to blend, adding slowly rest of olive oil until totally blended. Pour over each potato ball evenly. Garnish with lettuce leaves and sliced eggs, sprinkling parsley over the top. Serve cold.

Christmas Picnic

By Trinita Coris de Montalvo

Puerto Rico, the crossroads of the Caribbean, is a beautiful island belonging to the United States. Rio Piedras is a university town, the second in size. The university and its nearness to the capital have probably been the main reasons for the city's enormous growth in the last ten years. The First Baptist Church, located in the heart of the city, has the largest church membership on the island. It is a self-supporting church, and if it had a large enough building to accommodate all the people who want to come, it probably would be helping in the support of other smaller churches. As it is, its lay people keep thirteen outstations open, telling others the good news of salvation through faith in our Lord Jesus Christ.

It was a beautiful morning in December when a group of young people started from this church in two cars and two station wagons. They were taking a Christmas program to a church up in the hills. The air was cool and fresh. Laughter and song prevailed among them, wholesome laughter which is the result of joy found in the higher things of life. They passed the town of Caguas, then Gurabo. Farther on they left the cars on the road and climbed the steep hills on foot. The narrow trail took them to a wooden chapel on the mountain summit. They did not climb right up, however, but stopped at every house to sing some Christmas carols, read the Word and pray. Down into a glen, up again on the trail, up the hill, until finally they reached the chapel by noon.

In the yard, some of the members had prepared and were ready to serve a characteristic Christmas luncheon of *lechón asado* (roast pig) , *arroz* (rice), *gandinga* (stew), *plátanos asados y cocidos* (roasted and boiled plantains), *café y dulce* (coffee and candy).

The country women prepared this recipe for *gandinga* and the rest of the menu. It was lovingly served, by the young people of the church, to the group of young people from the church in the university town, most of whom were college students. Many of the rural youth had not been able to go beyond the lower grades in school, but that made no difference. All of them together offered the incense of their love, the gold of their youth, as they joined in singing the *villancicos* (Christmas carols), making true on His birthday the prayer He offered near His death:

"That they all may be one; as thou, Father, art in me, and I in thee, that they also may be one in us: that the world may believe that thou hast sent me."—*John* 17:21

When the sun began to set, the chapel bell merrily called the other church members, and they could be seen at a distance coming from all directions, carrying their torches with them for the return trip. These were not needed, for the moon shone that evening as it must have shone on that first Christmas night.

After giving the beautiful Christmas message in song and Scripture, the happy group started on the way home. As they watched a beautiful star — the Bethlehem star — they sang from the depth of their hearts, "Silent night! Holy night!"

PUERTO RICO

GANDINGA—stew

1 pound *gandinga:* pork liver	10 or 12 capers
or heart	¼ pound lard
1 small onion	⅛ pound bacon
2 small tomatoes	⅛ pound ham
1 green pepper	3 potatoes
3 sections garlic	1 small can tomato sauce
3 laurel leaves	4 tablespoons vinegar
10 or 12 small olives	

Clean the meat well. Scald the meat and throw the water away. Cut meat and other ingredients into small pieces. Brown meat, onion, peppers, crushed garlic, bacon and ham in lard. Add other ingredients and enough water not quite to cover. Season to taste and boil over a low fire until tender. Serves six.

Cazuela

Sweet Potato Pie

By Pia Cruz de Colon

Cook one and a half pounds of sweet potatoes and one pound of squash in salt water. Mash. Mix one cup of sugar, one teaspoon of cinnamon and one tablespoon of flour. Combine with mashed potato and squash. Beat three eggs. Mix with one cup of evaporated milk and two tablespoons of butter. Stir into potato and squash. Bake in a greased mold.

PUERTO RICO

Puerto Rico Special

By Lydia Huber

Arroz con dulce — sweet rice — is a national dish, always served at Christmas time and for any special occasion in the homes of the rich and the poor. My first months in Puerto Rico I was served this dish everywhere I went. The new missionary must be shown hospitality in the traditional way.

How well I remember entering homes so poor that not even a table or chair was in evidence. A crude stool was found for the missionary while the rest of the family squatted on the floor, and if they knew beforehand that I was coming then *arroz con dulce* was served on a plate with a native spoon made from a gourd. Etiquette, amongst the poor or wealthy, requires that a guest eat the food presented. I always ate it.

Many years later, I was taking some American friends calling. They were anxious to meet some of the families even in desperately poor homes. So that we would not surprise these people, I told them that I would be calling on them and bringing some friends with me. I selected four homes in which the families had suffered great hardship. In each home we were served *arroz con dulce*. It was made especially for us. Their sense of hospitality surmounted all other conditions. With only a few cents a day to live on, they managed to make this favorite dish for "the American guests."

Whenever I entertain *Puertoriqueños,* to please them I serve *arroz con dulce*. They are always so delighted when continentals serve a native dish. It proves that we like their food and that we like them.   PUERTO RICO

ARROZ CON DULCE—sweet rice

1 coconut	1 teaspoon ginger
1½ cups rice	1 teaspoon cloves
½ cup raisins	1 teaspoon salt
2 sticks of cinnamon	1 teaspoon butter

½ cup brown or ½ cup white sugar

Remove the brown skin on coconut meat, grate or put through the meat grinder. Extract the milk from the ground nut by pouring a little water over it and then pressing out the milk. There should be at least a cup of milk. Add the other ingredients to the milk and cook until rice is soft. Place in a dish and sprinkle with cinnamon.

Wedding Chocolate

By Margaret Mergal

I think that perhaps you would like to have typical recipes from Puerto Rico. I send "Wedding Chocolate" because this was served at our own wedding in Barranquitas. We had the reception at the home of one of our pioneer Christians. She prepared the traditional "chocolate" and I supplied the wedding cake and a toasted cake which comes in strips about three inches long. Of course, it seemed a bit strange to me that wedding guests should always expect to drink chocolate. Here, when the talk is about a forthcoming marriage, one will always hear the question, "¿Cuándo vamos a tomar chocolate?" (When are we going to be invited to drink chocolate?)

As you know, rice is the staple diet here. It is served twice a day, at lunch and dinner, with varying accompaniments such as red kidney beans, Spanish beans, codfish, or various meat dishes. I recall my amazement upon coming to Puerto Rico to find that what I had known all my life as "Spanish Rice" wasn't Spanish at all! Good rice here is dry, each kernel by itself, and it is good!

PUERTO RICO

WEDDING CHOCOLATE

½ pound grated chocolate
8 cups warm milk
2 beaten egg yolks
4 tablespoons butter
1 can (14 oz.) evaporated milk

Melt the chocolate and add the warm milk. Boil. Add evaporated milk and cook in double boiler. Before this reaches boiling point, add beaten yolks and butter. Remove from fire, and beat for two minutes. 12 to 15 cups.

CAZUELA—the pumpkin pie of Puerto Rico

2 cups mashed sweet potato
2 cups mashed squash
¼ cup rice flour
½ teaspoon salt
¾ cup sugar
2 teaspoons cinnamon
¾ teaspoon cloves
4 beaten eggs
1 cup of coconut milk (cow's milk may be used)

Mix potato and squash. Put through strainer to remove fibers. Add other ingredients in the order given. Bake in flat baking dish at 350 degrees for one hour. A cup of seedless raisins may be added before baking.

A Country Affair

By Petronila Nieves

This special dinner was given in honor of our chorus. It was celebrated in a country town called Mediania Alta, near Rio Grande. A good family gave their house for the celebration. The house was near the seashore.

It was a beautiful morning in the month of June. A bus was waiting for our chorus in front of the Christian Center. Everybody, thirty in number, took their seats in the bus, faces radiant with happiness.

We began our journey early in the morning. It looked beautiful, as are the mornings in Puerto Rico. We passed lovely scenery along the road; the flamboyants in blossom looked like red curtains on both sides of the road. The palm trees looked like big fans up in the mountains and down in the plain and valleys. We crossed a wide river, and there everything was so green, different shades in the grass and in the many kinds of trees. The birds were singing and flying in groups.

We left the principal road and took a narrow lane to Mediania Alta. The good family was waiting for us and gave us all the comfort they could so that we might spend a happy day. They even had for us all the coconut water we desired. All of us were happy roaming around the grounds and enjoying the beauty of God's creation. Later, we went to the seashore; some went bathing, others rested on the beach. At twelve o'clock we went back to the house for dinner.

"This is wonderful," said Carlos, one of our boys.

"Oh, yes," Raul agreed. "It is a great day for us, to eat such a good dinner under this old tree."

"We should do something like this often," said Juanita.

Before eating we had a prayer of gratitude for this opportunity that God gave to us of having this happy day. Then we ate under the shadow of the big tree at small tables.

Later, we had a special service with the family. Our chorus sang and read the Scripture and gave our testimony. We tried to demonstrate to this family our great gratitude to them. They were very kind to us.

At four o'clock we returned to San Juan, very happy.

PUERTO RICO

MENU

Roast pig   Boiled bananas

Rice with chicken   Rice with coconut

Coffee

ROAST PIG AS IT IS DONE IN THE COUNTRY

Prepare the pig the day before. Add salt and pepper and grease with *achiote* to give color. Put pig on a long stick, a spit. In a side yard of the house you can put two small sticks to hold the ends of the big stick the pig is on. Use charcoal or wood to roast it. It has to be turned constantly to prevent it from burning as it cooks through.

RICE WITH CHICKEN

8 pounds rice	½ pound tomatoes
2 Chickens, 2½ pounds each	1 quart olives
½ pound bacon	½ pound lard
½ pound ham	¼ pound garlic
½ pound onions	½ pound green peppers

Green leaves called *recao*

Prepare the chicken and cut in pieces. Fry bacon, ham and lard together. Fry onions, add tomatoes, garlic, olives, green leaves. Add chicken. Mix, cover and cook for 15 minutes. If chicken is soft, add the rice and stir. Add water and more grease. Cook on moderate fire until the rice is dry and soft. Use *achiote* or tomato sauce to give color to the rice.

RICE WITH COCONUT

2 pounds rice	1 pound sugar
1 coconut	1 pound raisins

Cinnamon and cloves

Put the rice to soften for some hours. Take out the coconut milk and add two liters (approximately two quarts) of water. Add ginger, sugar, cinnamon, cloves. Put on fire till it boils, add the rice and raisins, cook until the rice becomes dry and soft. Stir constantly for five minutes. Serve on small plates.

BOILED BANANAS

Cut 15 bananas in half, one half for each person. Boil in salty water until meat of banana is firm but soft.

The Gentlemen Did It

By INES F. QUILES

I think it is a fine idea to introduce people in different parts of the world to each other, to interpret land and customs as well as food and faith to other members of our Christian family.

Every organization in our church is carrying on some activity with which to raise funds to help in the payment of a debt to our Home Mission Society. This debt was incurred for the purpose of constructing a two-story building, the first floor to be used for our school and the second for our minister's home.

The gentlemen of our church wanted to make a special effort, so they prepared a banquet on September tenth. Although it was not a very large group that attended the banquet, it was splendid and an atmosphere of very beautiful Christian fraternity prevailed.

Speeches related to the activity and to the day school were delivered by friends of the church, members and our minister. Part of the menu served on this occasion were Rice and Chicken and *Postre Tembleque*.

PUERTO RICO

RICE AND CHICKEN

3 pounds chopped chicken
¼ ounce garlic
1 teaspoon black pepper
2 sweet red dwarf peppers
2 tablespoons salt
¾ pound ham chopped
2 ounces bacon chopped
4 ounces tomatoes

2 pimientos (2 ounces)
4 tablespoons lard
2 ounces onion
2 pounds rice
4 cups water
Salt at will
½ cup olives
2 tablespoons capers

Prepare the chicken the day before with salt, pepper, garlic and the sweet red dwarf peppers. Cook over a flame in a frying pan with ham, bacon, tomato sauce, pimientos and onion. Add the chicken and cook on a slow fire for about 30 minutes. Wash the rice, add the water and stir well. Cook rice on a slow fire and without cover. When water has evaporated, add olives and capers. Cover and cook now on a very slow fire. Stir several times before taking it off the flame. Garnish with seasoned peas and strips of pimientos. Ten servings.

POSTRE TEMBLEQUE—cornstarch pudding

¼ cup cornstarch
¼ cup sugar
1 teaspoon vanilla or a piece of lemon peel

4 cups coconut milk
¼ teaspoon salt

Mix the cornstarch with sugar and add the coconut milk. Add flavoring. Cook over a slow fire. Dust with cinnamon powder and serve. Eight servings.

Wedges for Friendship

By HELEN C. SCHMITZ

The children of Colegio Bautista put on a big "Welcoming Fiesta" when I visited their school. They wore Salvadorean Indian dress to put color and gaiety into the occasion. Many gifts expressed their welcome: sweets to express their love, flowers to represent the happy faces of the school children, handiwork to show the variety of Salvadorean ability, and many kinds of fruit so that when the visitor had eaten she would no longer feel strange but would be at home in beautiful El Salvador. The abundance of the fruit made it imperative that some of it be preserved. So it was that I ate my first delicious Salvadorean Wedge.

Colegio Bautista, a primary school for both boys and girls, was founded in 1924 by Miss Vivian Saylor, an American Baptist missionary. The school was started in the first place because Baptist children had rather a difficult time in the schools of the country. The fifty pupils of the first classes quickly grew into one hundred and crowded the Baptist church facilities. After eight years the school moved into "the palace," a beautiful structure built on the outskirts of San Salvador, the capital city. This was a project of the Golden Anniversary Fund of the Woman's American Baptist Home Mission Society.

The new building was far away from the center of things and as yet good transportation had not been instituted, so the school had to build a new constituency. At first only three rooms of the beautiful new building were needed. The school, however, quickly won a following and for many years has had a long waiting list. The psychological effect of this is to insure the maximum of co-operation from the student body. Colegio

Bautista had stood first in scholarship in the National examinations from the beginning.

Today discerning parents desire for their children the kind of moral and intellectual training the school gives, even though they do not want their children to take on Protestant ways of thinking. In registering his son, one father said to Miss McCutcheon, "I want you to have my son but I do not want you to teach him religion."

The principal replied, "Perhaps we had better not take him, then, for each of our pupils has a daily Bible class and goes daily to chapel."

"I know that," replied the father, "I just don't want you to teach him religion."

But the Bible teaches both civic virtue and spiritual values. This son eventually became a Baptist and his influence is wide, for he has a radio program, and contact with the government. So it is that a school serves as an opening WEDGE into a community that had been closed because of prejudice. Many alumni of the school are now serving in places of responsibility in the nation.

NEW YORK

SALVADOREAN PINEAPPLE WEDGES

½ cup vinegar
3 cups sugar
8 cloves

Cinnamon sticks
Preserved ginger
1 pineapple

1 lemon (juice and grated rind)

Cut pineapple into circles, peel and cut into pie shapes. Start ingredients cooking; place pineapple wedges in syrup and cook until fruit is clear, about 15 minutes. When cool, serve with dinner.

THE AMERICAS –
NORTH
AMERICA

Psalm 117

O praise the Lord, all ye nations:
    praise him, all ye people.
For his merciful kindness is great toward us:
    and the truth of the Lord endureth for ever.
        Praise ye the Lord.

Scripture Cake and Preserve!

By HELEN M. WIGGINTON

When I was about to marry Frank, Mother Wigginton gave me a cookbook, a printed one, in which she said she had written two very important recipes that she hoped I would use often. Upon looking in the "Cake" section of the cookbook I found in her dear old-fashioned writing, *Scripture Cake*. Further on in the section, "Canning, Preserving and Pickling," I found a recipe on *How to Preserve a Husband*. I am most happy to share these with you and with others, for they have meant very much to me for twenty-five years.   PENNSYLVANIA

SCRIPTURE CAKE

1 cup butter—Judges 5:25
3½ cups flour (prepared) —
1 Kings 4:22
1 cup almonds—Genesis
43:11
1 cup water—Genesis 24:20
A little salt—Leviticus 2:13

2 cups sugar—Jeremiah 6:20
2 cups raisins—1 Samuel 30:12
2 cups figs—1 Samuel 30:12
6 eggs—Isaiah 10:14
Sweet spices to taste—1 Kings
10:2

Follow Solomon's advice for making good boys—first clause of Proverbs 23:14—and you will have a good cake. You can add citron if you like.

HOW TO PRESERVE A HUSBAND

Be careful in your selection.

Do not choose too young or green, and take only such as have been reared in good moral atmosphere.

When once decided upon and selected, turn your thoughts to preparation for domestic use.

Some insist upon keeping them in a pickle, while others are constantly putting them in hot water. This only makes them sour, hard and sometimes bitter. Even poor varieties may be made sweet, tender and good by garnishing them with patience, well-sweetened with smiles and flavored with kisses to taste. Then wrap them in a mantle of charity, keep with a steady fire of domestic devotion, and serve with peaches and cream.

When thus prepared they will keep for years. —FANNIE C. WIGGINTON

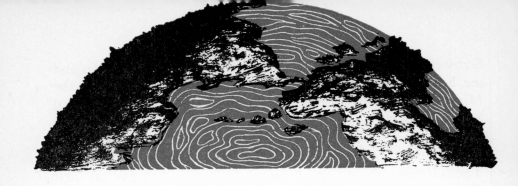

Easter at Home

By ZELMA F. STONE

SETTING: It is Easter Sunday at Doane Cottage, Kodiak Baptist Mission. Twelve Alaskan Aleut children and two servicemen are around the table with the missionary house parents. The centerpiece on the table is a tall, round *Koolich* surrounded by colored Easter eggs.

MENU: Ham, sweet potatoes, green vegetables, cole slaw, pineapple sherbet with *Koolich*

CONVERSATION

Older child: When we had *Koolich* at home, we put it in the Holy Corner by the icons and didn't eat any until after the Russian priest came and blessed it. Then it was served with tea to any guests that came.

Another child: We always carried an Easter egg with us when we left our homes on Easter Sunday. When we met someone, we said, "Christ is risen" (in Russian), and exchanged eggs.

Another child: Yes, and sometimes by the end of the day we would have the same egg we started out with.

Four-year-old: I know why Jesus died on the cross.

Older child: Why?

Four-year-old (seriously): So He could be a rose.

Seven-year-old: The women went to the cave where they put Jesus and cried because they didn't know He would live again. I remember when we lived at home we went to the Russian church on Saturday night to kiss pictures of Jesus and Mary.

Serviceman: What a joy it is to be here with these children and see how happy they are. It isn't only the children that the Mission helps. I remember the day I came in from the Naval Station, looked in the windows of the many bars as I walked through Kodiak and was about to enter one so I could forget my homesickness for my own children and family at home. Then I remembered the Mission and came out for my first visit. I have had many happy hours of Christian fellowship out here since that day, and I shall never cease to be thankful that I found the Mission before it was too late and renewed my fellowship with Christians and my Lord. Now I have the courage to witness for Him to those I work with and have introduced many other homesick servicemen to the Mission where they, too, have spent many happy wholesome hours.

ALASKA

KOOLICH—Russian Easter bread

This is Russian Easter bread. I have used the spelling that I found on the handwritten recipe that I presume was from a native.

The bread is baked in round three-pound shortening tins, No. 10 cans or tall juice cans. After baking, it is frosted all over with powdered-sugar icing and decorated with multicolored decorettes.

1 quart milk, lukewarm	1 pound melted butter
1 quart water, lukewarm	1 pound raisins
2 packages dry yeast	1 teaspoon vanilla extract
3½ cups sugar	1 teaspoon lemon extract
¼ cup salt	Spices and caraway seed
11 eggs	Flour to beat

1 pound walnuts or almonds or fruitcake mix

Dissolve the yeast in lukewarm liquid. When it begins to work, add sugar, salt and beaten eggs. Add enough flour to make a paste and beat with whisk or spoon until the lumps disappear. Add melted shortening, when it is lukewarm, and remaining ingredients. Add just enough flour so that it will knead well. Place in a greased pan and let rise until double in bulk. Divide into loaves and let rise in the tins. Bake in moderate oven (350-375°) for one hour or until done. Place cooky sheet on proper rack of oven to keep the loaves from burning.

111

saw a cross while the raindrops glisten in what the sun provides?
but the no it cares vanish and rises go up to pray for a day for improving
the next day.

First Baptist Barbecue

By ROSE FETZ

It was in 1949 that the annual First Baptist barbecue was organized to interest our people in the possibilities of the Baptist Center grounds. The property includes approximately seven acres. It has a ball field, well grassed, with lights that make it possible to use in night games and for recreation of many kinds.

The Scout building, built almost entirely by volunteer labor, has a kitchen with gas stove, two rest rooms, a fireplace (did you see the cross in the center?) made of rock which was hauled from the northern part of the state "for free." It is the type that can be chiseled into almost any form for decorative purposes. There is a grill for outdoor cooking and, of course, the barbecue pit which is three feet wide, five feet long and six feet deep.

There is quite a ceremony when the people gather round the covered pit and wait for the tarpaulins to be pulled back, the earth shoveled away and another layer of tarpaulin removed. Next, boards are dug out with great ceremony, and the odor of well-done beef reaches the nostrils even before the eyes spy out the great chunks of beef deep in the pit. Huge pieces are forked onto tremendous iron pans. At last the carving begins! Long lines of people are served the beef quickly; then they seek out the less important but also flavorsome parts of the feast.

It is always such a satisfaction to watch the fellowship of a barbecue group moving about, talking, laughing, so full of their own barbecued beef they are mellow. The program is never long, and the ball game finds a vociferous gang to cheer or razz the players. The majority go home anticipating next year's event while the committee groans in relief because another barbecue is safely past and tries to get inspiration for improving the next one.

ARIZONA

BARBECUE MENU
Barbecued beef

Green salad   Pinto beans   French bread

Coffee

Ice cream   Soft drinks

BARBECUED BEEF
200 pounds of whole chuck beef—leave bones in for flavor.

Cut meat into about 20 pound chunks; rub in salt (1 pound salt to 1 ounce pepper). Wrap each chunk in paper—lettuce packing paper holds the juice. A burlap sack soaked in water is wrapped around the paper, and each chunk is wire-tied before being lowered into the pit (this makes it easy to lift in and out).

Start the fire in the pit about three hours before meat is put into it. Use firewood that makes good coals. There must be 18 inches of coals before a 50-pound bag of oak charcoal is added. When all wood particles have ceased flaming and the entire bed is red hot coals, place grill over coals, cover with wet burlap which has been wrung out, place meat bundles on grill. Cover the pit with boards, cover boards with a heavy tarpaulin and cover tarpaulin with dirt until no trace of escaping steam can be seen. This latter must all be done very quickly to avoid losing heat and to prevent any steam escaping. Leave for 24 hours. Uncover, unwrap and serve with barbecue sauce. Serves 300 people.

We buy the barbecue sauce by the gallon and dilute about half.

113

For Food and Friends, and All Good Things

By A. May Hill

We sat at a long table in the Christian Center parlor. The freshly painted pale green walls of the room and the new cream-tone draperies on the windows gave a pleasurable setting for our dinner party. These details, however, were scarcely noticed because of the gaiety around the candlelighted table. The table was really beautiful! Light green candles in yellow lacy holders, and a gorgeous center arrangement of yellow chrysanthemums, soft-toned tuberous begonias of many hues and maidenhair fern enhanced the table. Soft lighting in the room and soft, sweet music from the radio completed the atmosphere of thorough enjoyment.

The group at the table were Spanish-speaking men and women, with the exception of a staff member of the Center. Everything about the party seemed to bear witness of happiness and gratitude, for this was the Thanksgiving season. Thanksgiving was in the air, in hearts, and smiles and words!

"What are you most thankful for?" soon became a topic of conversation. We thought and talked together of our common blessings of food, friends and home. Soon we were expressing heartfelt thankfulness for our wonderful heritage of Christian ideals and ideas, all sacred to us.

Mrs. Dee again drew our attention with her sparkling dark eyes and radiant smile. She already had entertained us with several hymns, some of which she sang in Spanish and others in English.

"I am so very thankful," she said, "that I know how to talk

114

to God. I don't need to have someone else pray to God for me. I talk to my heavenly Father myself, in the name of my Savior, Jesus Christ. This makes me feel so very happy and thankful!"

Someone at the table told of being in a group of Japanese girls who came from a Buddhist background. Their club met at the Christian Center each Saturday morning, and among other hymns which they sang they always chose the "Battle Hymn of the Republic" — "Mine Eyes Have Seen the Glory of the Coming of the Lord." At the last verse the leader asked, "What does Christ mean to you?"

One girl replied, "Oh, about the same as Buddha," but another girl spoke up quickly, "I know what He means to me. I am a Christian!" The glow on her face and in her eyes told what was in her heart. "Yes, Christians know that Jesus died for us. Did Buddha do that?"

And so, on and on around the long table there were expressions of faith, of joy and of gratitude for our Christian heritage. Are we not all grateful for FOOD, CHRISTIAN FELLOWSHIP and our FREEDOM THROUGH CHRIST!

CALIFORNIA

MENU

Ripe Olives	Celery
Gallina en Mole—Chicken in Chili	Chicken à la King—Spanish style

Pickles

Tortillas	Spanish Rice

Strawberry Jello and Whipped Cream or Apple Pie

Coffee

GALLINA EN MOLE—chicken in chili
Mole or red chili sauce

½ cup almonds	2 tablespoons flour
¼ cup raisins	1 teaspoon salt
3 cloves garlic	2 tablespoons chili powder
1 small onion	½ teaspoon anise seed
½ cup fat	2 cups meat broth or hot water

Put almonds, raisins, garlic and onions through food chopper. Brown in 2 tablespoons of hot fat. Add other ingredients, except meat, and stir until smooth. Cook 20 minutes.

Cut chicken into as small pieces as possible (with bone in), cover with water, boil until tender, drain, roll in flour. Brown in remaining hot fat, place in saucepan and cover with *mole*. Add enough broth or hot water to cover, cook one hour. Stir occasionally to keep from sticking. Pour entire mixture into dish for serving.

(Turkey, fowl or any kind of meat may be used with *Mole*.) If using meat, cut into pieces about 2 x 2 inches.

CHICKEN A LA KING

3 or 4 pound chicken	2 cups milk
1 cup ready-mix pancake flour	4 stalks celery (3-inch lengths)
1 teaspoon salt	¼ chopped green pepper
1 teaspoon pepper	1 can cream of mushroom soup

Wash chicken; dry; disjoint. Add salt and pepper to pancake flour and mix. Roll chicken in flour and fry in fat or salad oil one inch deep letting it turn to brown. Cover and cook slowly about twenty-five minutes. Take out pieces and drain on paper. Drain fat from pan, saving one tablespoon for gravy. To the one tablespoon of fat add leftover flour and one cup milk. Mix well. Add the celery, green pepper and chicken, slowly. Cook 10 minutes. Remove celery. Add one can of mushroom soup and remainder of milk. Cook slowly for another ten minutes, stirring occasionally. Pour the entire mixture of chicken and gravy into a large bowl or dish. It is now ready to serve.

TORTILLAS

3 pounds ripe corn	3 quarts water
3 ounces quick lime	1 tablespoon fat for griddle frying

Put corn into iron pot, add lime and water to cover corn. Boil until corn begins to peel. Remove from fire and let cool. Rub corn between hands until skins and kernel separate, then rinse in cold water until corn is white. This is called *nixtamol*. Run through food chopper several times until the *nixtamol* is a fine, soft dough. This dough is called *masa*. Shape *masa* into cakes five inches in diameter, pat out very thin. Bake on lightly greased griddle, turning frequently to brown evenly and slightly. Serve hot.

Tortillas are used as bread. No butter is necessary.

116

A Chung Mei Tidbit

By EDWARD H. TONG

My intention was to consult my wife's mother and obtain some unique Chinese dish for you. However, upon further thought, perhaps many of the ingredients would be too difficult to obtain to be of any practical value. Here is a recipe that can be made use of very easily. It is for Sweet Potato Puffs, one of the many sweetmeats traditionally made around this time of the year since it is Chinese New Year. It is known and greatly enjoyed by the boys at Chung Mei.

CALIFORNIA

SWEET POTATO PUFFS, CANTONESE

2 pounds sweet potatoes
1 cup glutinous rice flour, or
   1 cup of pastry flour

1 cup dark brown sugar
¼ cup sesame seeds, or ½ cup
   coarse-ground peanuts

Peel and boil sweet potatoes. Drain well, mash and season lightly with salt. Mix in flour until potatoes are of a doughlike consistency. Flour hands and pat dough into flat cakes. Dab on each 1 teaspoon of brown sugar. Cup hands around the cakes and form into balls. Shredded coconut or preserved watermelon rind might be used as a tasty center for the puff. Roll these balls in sesame seed or in the ground peanuts. Fry in deep fat until the potato puffs are deep brown.

Food For Funds

By Tsutomu Fukuyama

This *suki-yaki* dinner was prepared at the request of the Church of the Brethren, Denver, and served to a group of seventy-five members as a money-raising project for funds for the International Christian University in Tokyo, Japan.

The term *suki-yaki* literally means broiling or baking on a spade. We are told that the Japanese peasant would cook his noon meal, of vegetables gathered from the field and meat brought from home, on his spade, *suki*. In Japanese homes today the meal is cooked at the dinner table, with a good deal of ceremony, often on a small charcoal burner.

COLORADO

SUKI-YAKI—spade broil

Apparently there is no specific formula for the meal, although one should follow a certain procedure in cooking it. The following will serve five:

1½ pounds lean beef, cut in paper-thin pieces	1 soy bean cake
1 small stalk celery, cut in bite sizes	1 pound bean sprouts
6 bunches green onions, cut in bite sizes (or several round onions, sliced)	3 tablespoons sugar
Stalks of greens: Chinese cabbage or spinach	½ cup soy sauce
	½ cup water

Fry the thin pieces of beef in a small amount of shortening until browned. Add sugar and soy sauce diluted with the water. Add vegetables, all of which have been cut into bite-sizes. Simmer for short time, 5 to 7 minutes. *Suki-yaki* is better if the vegetables are slightly undercooked than if they are overcooked.

After washing one pound of rice several times, add 2 cups of water. Soak for 15 minutes. Place on high heat and cook until rice boils. Lower heat and simmer rice for 15 minutes. Remove rice from heat, but leave cover on saucepan additional 10 minutes for best flavor.

Other vegetables may be used in the *suki-yaki*, such as carrots, cauliflower, string beans, either in addition to or in place of those given in this recipe.

If dessert is desired, raw fruit or plain cookies may be used.

For Simple Things

By MABEL G. BAILEY

In early Quaker days plain clothes were worn in a protest against the waste involved in following the caprices of fashion. Later, the Quaker garb was "simple" only in appearance; it necessitated a good deal more expenditure of time and money than clothes made for non-Quaker neighbors. When knee breeches were generally discarded for trousers, most Quaker men finally made the change. In one meeting, in fact, there was only one man left who wore knee breeches. One woman Friend rejoiced in his devotion to the old ways, beginning her sermon with these words: "It delights my heart that there is still amongst us a precious remnant in breeches."

CONNECTICUT

CASSEROLE OF ASPARAGUS AND EGGS

1 can asparagus   4 sliced hard-boiled eggs

Place in layers with two cups cream sauce poured over all. Cover with buttered crumbs. Bake at 375° until brown.

Good Americans

By ALMA G. BROADHEAD

Many years ago, when I was working in the coal and coke district of southwestern Pennsylvania, I was invited into a Hungarian home for supper after Sunday school held in the afternoon. The parents had not been in America long, and they idolized their little daughter, Katie, since their other six children had died in babyhood. The father, mother, Katie and I sat down to a chicken dinner. A big piece of white meat was in the center of a large plate of soup at my place. Katie asked for the head when her mother served us. She was quietly admonished to be still, and a drumstick placed in her plate. She quickly ate it and again asked for the head but received a generous helping of white meat. When that had disappeared, Katie said in a determined tone, "Now, Mom, this is the third time I'm asking for the head, and I *want* it this time."

With a helpless, apologetic glance at me, the mother lifted from the soup pot the cooked head of the fowl, replete with comb. As Katie dug out an eye and popped it into her mouth, she sighed in ecstasy, "M-m-m. I do think chicken is the best meat there is; the head is the best part of the chicken, and the eye is the best part of the head!"

Then my hostess told me, in very broken English, she had asked her neighbor how to make an apple pie and, in my honor, had baked her first one. The whole family glowed with pride and satisfaction as she served a quarter of it to each of us. The crust was very "long" and thick and the filling of apples very thin, but I choked it down with the feeling that, with the serving of this typical American dessert, the members of this family were dedicating themselves to our national customs and ideals.

120

Broken Muffins

By Alma G. Broadhead

The greatest inspiration I received last year was in one of my cooking classes, composed that night of six boys and two girls. They had just made their first muffins. They gazed at the muffins silently, almost reverently, and, as we sat around the table waiting for them to cool, they were strangely thoughtful. Instead of the usual blessing we said together, I was led to pray our thanks for allowing food to grow and for giving us skill to prepare it, closing with our gratitude for our Father's willingness and ability to meet all our needs. When the muffins were broken, it almost seemed as though we were at the Communion table.

As each piece had a bit of butter placed on it and eaten, loud satisfaction was expressed at its goodness. Each one had two and was careful to take one home to Mother.

CONNECTICUT

MUFFINS

½ cup all purpose flour
⅔ teaspoon baking powder
¼ teaspoon salt
1 scant tablespoon sugar
¼ egg
½ tablespoon melted fat
¼ cup milk

Sift the four dry ingredients together. Add the beaten egg and melted fat to the milk, and stir this mixture quickly into the dry ingredients. Do not over-mix. About ¼ minute will leave the batter rough. Drop with spoon into 4 muffin tins. Bake at 425° F. for about 20 minutes. Yield—4 muffins.

(To divide an egg, beat it till foamy, and divide with a spoon.)

RIN TUM DITTY

Each group of two would make this. All liked it, and many later told me they were making it frequently for their noon lunch.

Heat ⅓ can cream of tomato soup. Cut in cubes ⅛ pound of cheese. Let it melt in soup over slow fire. Pour over crackers or buttered toast.

A Canadian Sweet

By ROSALIE OLSON

During one summer, when I helped with the cooking at the Baptist Missionary Training School in Chicago, one of our Canadian girls, Ernestina Schmidt, made a delicious dessert and taught me how to make it. Very good!

ILLINOIS

CANADIAN GRAHAM CRACKER DESSERT

Mix the following ingredients and cool before using:

½ pound chopped dates
½ cup cold water
2 tablespoons brown sugar

Rind ½ orange, grated
2 tablespoons orange juice
1 teaspoon lemon juice

Lay 2 or 3 or 4 whole graham crackers on a plate as the first layer. Spread mixture. Add crackers and mixture alternately, using 4, 5 or 6 layers of crackers. Frost with powdered sugar. Let stand a few hours and then slice.

Christian Fellowship

By ALICE F. SNAPE

It was Mr. F's birthday! We were welcomed into their spacious living room in one of our Chicago suburbs. The young folks entertained us by singing, playing the electric organ, the baby grand piano, the electric vibraharp, the violin, the marimba. You know the family is musical!

About forty guests were invited to the dining room. Pink candles, flowers, delicate Chinese china and such food adorned the table! Most of the Chinese delicacies were made by Mrs. F., with the assistance of their college-age daughter and high school son. It is hard to say which Chinese dish was best! I liked especially the sweet-sour spareribs.

After the delightful feast and watching television, we felt we would never want anything more to eat, but strange to say none of us felt "stuffed" as we do after an American dinner. At last we returned to the living room while the young people cleared the table and washed the dishes in the electric dishwasher! Some of the guests went downstairs to view pictures in the playroom and to see the display, in miniature, of the Chicago 1933-1934 "Century of Progress," a hobby of our host. Finally, according to the daily custom of the family, we all gathered for devotions. A chapter from the Bible was read and a page of *The Secret Place*, a prayer was offered and was followed by all uniting in praying the Lord's Prayer and singing the Doxology. This was a fitting climax to an unforgettable evening of Christian fellowship.

ILLINOIS

SWEET-SOUR SPARERIBS

1 large can cubed pineapple	¼ or ½ cup vinegar
2½ or 3 pounds spareribs	¼ cup granulated sugar
2 tablespoons cornstarch	3 tablespoons Chinese sauce

Cut spareribs into small pieces and brown in a large frying pan, using a little oil. Pour off excess grease. Mix pineapple juice from can, cornstarch, vinegar, sugar, and Chinese sauce (soy sauce). Thin with about 1 cup of water. Pour over spareribs. Cook till thick, like gravy. Last, add the pineapple cubes and serve with rice. This will serve 6 people. Other vegetable dishes should be served at the same meal.

Bobsledding in Iowa

By Alice C. Brown

At seven o'clock the bobsled was gotten ready for the ride, given once or twice during the winter when the snow was good and the weather not too cold in northwest Iowa. The schoolmates and others had been chosen and invited personally. The bob was piled with straw and bedding. When we were ready to start, twenty-five or thirty boys and girls had been gathered up and were trying to get themselves comfortably located for the two- or three-hour ride. What squealing when the horses settled into a fast trot!

After riding far enough to be cold and tired, we turned toward our home where we knew the hot oyster soup and popcorn balls would be ready.

It took but little time for us to arrange ourselves, standing around the table — not room enough for sitting — with a good sized bowl of soup for each one, a heaping bowl of crackers, hot from the oven, and another bowl of hot, syrupy popcorn balls. There was plenty for all, with no restrictions against seconds or even thirds, until none wished for more.

Then another ride, until all, or nearly so, were ready for bed. Soon each child was delivered to his own home. No one of that group needed to be rocked to sleep that night!

OKLAHOMA

OYSTER SOUP

Put 4 gallons of fresh, sweet milk into a large pan which is put on the stove, where it will not get hot too quickly and scorch.

2 to 3 quarts of fresh oysters—enough for oyster soup for 20 to 30 children. Fry briefly in butter and oyster broth. Boil in milk. Add salt, pepper, butter in generous quantities. Add ¼ cup A-1 sauce. Sprinkle each dishful with paprika. Salty, crisp crackers. Popcorn, with plenty of butter and salt, made into popcorn balls; use Caro Corn Syrup.

New Year's Eve

By Marjorie A. Kenneally

On New Year's Eve I had supper and spent the evening in Wollaston, Massachusetts, in the home of Dr. and Mrs. "Higgie" Higginbotham. Before supper, we sat in the living room by the fireplace and looked at Christmas cards, listened to the murmuring fire in the fireplace, enjoyed the sparkling Christmas tree with its plastic star on the highest twig and the little crèche on the mantle that, through the years, has watched the Higginbotham children grow up. The cards came from all corners: a Japanese card; a card from Chicago, from the Baptist Missionary Training School; a Christmas letter from missionaries in Japan; a card from Evelyn Ma, adopted daughter of one of the China missionaries; another from "The Little Shepherdess" at our office, and many others.

After supper, we had an evening of poetry and prose. I will quote from Dr. Higginbotham's New Year message:

"The reason many of us are already disillusioned about the New Year is because we lack the power to achieve our highest and truest selves. That need not be. We, too, can say with Paul, 'I can do all things through Christ which strengtheneth me.' Don't misunderstand Paul or the speaker. It will take all the strength of heart and soul and mind and will that you can muster to become victorious personalities. You yourselves will have to do the things that need to be done, but you will have mighty reinforcements, for the illimitable power of God will be yours."   Massachusetts

SUPPER SNACK

The snack consisted of a slice of bread, a slice of cheese on top of the bread, two slices of tomato on top of this, topped by two strips of bacon. Arrange snack on broiler, and broil until heated through and toasted. M-m-m!

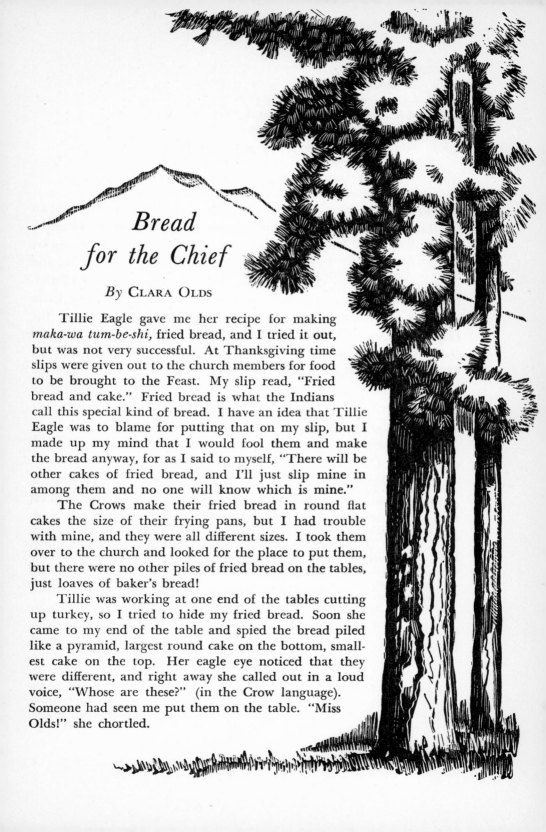

Bread
for the Chief

By Clara Olds

Tillie Eagle gave me her recipe for making
maka-wa tum-be-shi, fried bread, and I tried it out,
but was not very successful. At Thanksgiving time
slips were given out to the church members for food
to be brought to the Feast. My slip read, "Fried
bread and cake." Fried bread is what the Indians
call this special kind of bread. I have an idea that Tillie
Eagle was to blame for putting that on my slip, but I
made up my mind that I would fool them and make
the bread anyway, for as I said to myself, "There will be
other cakes of fried bread, and I'll just slip mine in
among them and no one will know which is mine."

The Crows make their fried bread in round flat
cakes the size of their frying pans, but I had trouble
with mine, and they were all different sizes. I took them
over to the church and looked for the place to put them,
but there were no other piles of fried bread on the tables,
just loaves of baker's bread!

Tillie was working at one end of the tables cutting
up turkey, so I tried to hide my fried bread. Soon she
came to my end of the table and spied the bread piled
like a pyramid, largest round cake on the bottom, small-
est cake on the top. Her eagle eye noticed that they
were different, and right away she called out in a loud
voice, "Whose are these?" (in the Crow language).
Someone had seen me put them on the table. "Miss
Olds!" she chortled.

Tillie's ample body shook with mirth as she went back to her task. She did not forget the white woman's attempt to make Indian bread, for whenever a new group came into the room, she marched to the other end of the tables, stabbed one of my fried bread cakes with her butcher knife, held it aloft like a war trophy and cried *"Ick-jak* (look), Miss Olds' *maka-wa tum-be-shi!"* and much merriment ensued.

The end was not yet. No one else had been told to bring fried bread. Mine was conspicuous not only because of the varied sizes of the cakes, but because they were the only ones on the whole long table of good things to eat.

The final laugh, however, was mine. It so happened that Plenty Coups, the Tribal Chief, was at the hospital after an operation on his eyes. Someone brought him over to the church for the Thanksgiving feast, and he was given a place of honor at a table set on the platform. No sooner had the blessing been asked than I heard him say, *"Maka-wa tum-be-shi sho?"* (Where's the fried bread?) The only fried bread at the feast was mine, so the missionary's Indian bread fed the Indian Chief. His eyes were bandaged so he could not see the peculiar shapes of the bread, but it must have tasted pretty good, even though made by a white woman.

MONTANA

MAKA-WA TUM-BE-SHI

1 cup (sifted) flour	½ teaspoon salt
1 rounded teaspoon baking powder	¾ cup water (warm or cold)

Mix all ingredients together, adding a little flour to keep dough from sticking to the hands. Form into a ball, then flatten out by patting with hands and turning from one hand to the other, until dough is about the size of the frying pan to be used. With knife or finger, make hole in the center of cake.

Have melted fat (lard, Crisco or other shortening) in pan, to depth of about ½ inch. It should be smoking hot before the cake is eased into it. Dough will puff up on top. When brown on other side, turn with fork and brown top side. When done, with fingers pull apart into pieces the desired size for serving. Butter, jelly or jam goes very well with this. One cake, frying-pan size, serves two or three persons.

Squaw Bread

By ANNA F. PETZOLDT

We were introduced to squaw bread when we were initiated as guests at a Crow Indian feast, fifty years ago. It is still being served as a special treat, when the Indian family is alone or on holidays.

At Christmas, especially, the missionaries are given this item by a couple of women who are adept in the art of preparation. Some years ago, the Advisory Board or Crow Christian Council, as it was later named, was organized as a training school to develop a native leadership. Usually there is a supper meeting. Each family brings a designated article of food — meat, vegetables, salad, bread or rolls, jelly, pickles, and dessert.

Occasionally someone brings a surprise item. In season, it may be baked pheasant, and often a stack of "squaw bread."

The purpose of the supper is fellowship. It is followed by a business and devotional program. The presiding officer is an Indian leader, previously chosen. After the table is cleared and dishes washed (in this the men as well as women take turns), each occupies his or her place at table for the devotional, in which each of the twenty-two members takes part. This monthly or bi-monthly meeting has been an important feature in Christian training and has developed a leadership of which any church could be proud.

Many of the Indian women are excellent cooks. They often prepare the new dishes better than the ones who give them recipes.

MONTANA

SQUAW BREAD

2 cups all purpose flour   1 scant teaspoon salt
4 teaspoons baking powder   ½ cup milk
½ cup water

Sift dry ingredients into a mixing bowl. Make a "well" in same and pour in liquid. Stir gradually until of a consistency to handle without sticking to hand. For this a little more flour may be needed; but dough should not be too stiff or bread will be tough. Divide into mounds the size of biscuits. Then with hands or rolling pin shape into flat cakes about size and thickness of baked pancakes. Cut slit in center to fry evenly. Have a griddle ready with deep hot shortening. Gently slide an uncooked flat piece into hot fat and fry until golden brown. Turn and finish each one until all are fried. Stack and keep hot until ready to serve.

They are really delicious served hot with syrup and coffee or as a bread item with any family meal. For variety a heaping tablespoon of sugar may be added to batter, a few raisins or nut meats, also a tablespoon of shortening.

—AGNES DEER NOSE

Sunday Fritters

By Anna F. Petzoldt

Living beyond reach of the corner grocery, and too far for walking distance, I have found it advisable to keep on hand a small stock of canned and packaged food supplies. These are for reserves — not to be used in daily food preparation.

When unexpected guests are to be entertained and a hurried meal must be prepared I like to serve salmon fritters with a lemon slice and parsley. They go well with tomato juice cocktail; creamed potatoes; a green tossed salad; hot rolls, either raised or baking powder; halved grapefruit with maraschino cherry and coffee.

Many charming guests have joined us in delightful spiritual fellowship around this simple repast.

Montana

SALMON FRITTERS

One can of salmon. Remove bones and skin. Add 3 eggs and 1 tablespoon of pimento or green pepper cut in small pieces.

Mix thoroughly. Drop by tablespoon in skillet into 2 tablespoons of hot bacon drippings. Fry to a delicate brown, turn, and finish. Serve hot, garnished with lemon slices, parsley sprigs or a cream sauce topping.

Food for Thought

By R. Dean Goodwin

I think it important that we not give the impression that we eat well on the mission field. I remember two meals particularly that I have eaten on the mission field.

One of the meals that sticks in my mind was in a pastor's home in Puerto Rico. The fare was simple, and the thing that impressed me was that here was a Christian home where they ate like Christians. You know, there is a difference between the way Christians eat and the way the others eat in Puerto Rico.

The other meal that I remember was in Dondon, Haiti, where the meal was served in a room that had no floor except the dirt. The meal was cooked out-of-doors. I do not remember the ingredients of it but I remember the situation. I think that such meals are more important to report than some of the delicious desserts that I had in hotels in Santiago.

I have no ear for recipes and therefore I could not tell you what was served at those meals. But I sincerely hope that, when people sit down to eat chicken in churches, they might remember meals served in rooms with dirt floors in Haiti.

NEW JERSEY

Baseball and Brotherhood

By Nora Jiles Hill

It was a crisp October afternoon, the closing day of the baseball season. The two top teams in the National League were playing an extra play-off game to break the tie that would decide which one of them would play the New York Yankees in the World Series.

What tension! What excitement in the Minot household whose members were ardent baseball fans.

The Minots—Fred, Susan and their son, Bruce—who live in Harlem in New York City, had invited guests, many of them foreign students studying in the city, to an early supper in order to share with them some of the excitement of the baseball game.

The guests gathered at the table, and Fred Minot began to say the grace. "Our Father," Susan's heart began to sing with special praise and thanksgiving, "for Bruce, our Father, that he is privileged to know early in his life the loveliness of so many of Thy children." And well could she be thankful, for at the table were: Leila from Egypt, Milos from Czechoslovakia, L.K. from India, Waka from Japan, Ato from South Africa, Chen from China; Ann of English, German, French and Irish descent, whose family had been in America for three hundred years, who came from the middle western part of our country, for her ancestors had gone west from New England in the covered wagon era; Grace, whose grandfather had been a slave in the South; Benjamin from Kentucky, and Kreig of the Jewish faith.

Halfway through the supper, the radio announcer cried out: "This is it. The Dodgers have won the pennant!" The forks of every American at the table were suspended in midair, and for a moment there was breathless silence and then a chorus of glad cheers. L.K. from India must have voiced the question in the minds of the other guests from abroad when he quietly asked: "Is this cheering you are doing a part of what some people call a bit of 'American madness'?"

"Yes," Susan replied, "and there are perhaps fifty million enjoying this same 'American madness' at this very moment."

Waka said, "I'd like to see our best Japanese team play your top American teams. We do rather well, you know."

Ato with sadness in his voice said: "We do not have ball parks for my people in South Africa. I am sure you are reading in the papers about segregation in my country."

Most of the guests expressed a desire to see a ball game. John Minot said that, if the series extended over more than four games, he could get tickets for them. Ato, L.K., Flo, Leila and Waka said they could arrange their school schedules so that they could attend a game.

Bruce grew ecstatic about the hot dogs, ice cream and soda pop at the baseball park but Milos demurred, "Bruce, your ball park menu leaves me cold. The food we had tonight is the most exciting I've eaten in my three years in America. Mrs. Minot, please give me the names of these dishes and tell me how they are prepared."

So Susan gave Milos, the Czechoslovakian guest, the menu and recipe for this real American supper.

Chilled Canned Apple Juice

Waffles   Creamed Chicken

Fresh Fruit Salad

Cottage Cheese Dressing

Coffee   Milk

Then she said, "We Americans have been making so much baseball noise that our guests haven't had a chance to express themselves. Benjamin, the piano is yours. Let's all sing."

Benjamin laughed as he moved toward the piano, "I always sing better on a full waffle stomach." With his rich baritone voice, he sang a Negro Spiritual, then a Kentucky mountain folk song. Kreig did a Hebrew lament; L.K. sang an Indian love song. One by one the other guests began to sing the songs of their own lands and all joined in the choruses.

Ann began to hum softly, " 'When we get to Heaven we going to sing a new song.' No," she said, "we don't want to wait to get to Heaven to sing our new song. We have been singing our new song of Brotherhood here tonight!"

NEW YORK

WAFFLES

2 cups flour	3 beaten egg yolks
4 tablespoons sugar	1½ cups milk
3 teaspoons baking powder	½ cup melted shortening
½ teaspoon salt	3 beaten egg whites

Mix and sift dry ingredients. Add egg yolks and milk. Then add melted shortening. Fold in egg whites. Bake until golden brown in color.

134

A Norwegian Tradition

By Alberta L. Kilmer

How easily traditions grow! A few years ago, my sister entertained her Circle at their Christmas meeting. Her mother-in-law is Norwegian; she helped to prepare the Norwegian refreshments that were served.

The next year I became co-hostess, and part of the meeting was held in my half of our two-family house. The piano was in my apartment, so we sang carols.

One year the devotional leader told a story of the manger scene. A crèche was used as a worship center. Since then, this has become the focal point of the Christmas decorations.

Another year we heard the story of "The Carol That Never Was Sung," a song of brotherhood that has not yet been realized. We added a small Christmas tree, trimmed by the flags of the United Nations, with a star at the top to symbolize the Christ.

Each year our fellowship grows wider, deeper, more significant than the year before. Devotions differ. The carols may be new. The manner of distributing gifts may be changed. But the refreshments are always the same, always delicious, always Norwegian. They have become a beautiful tradition.

NEW YORK

SANDKAKER

THE COOKIES

½ pound butter
1 cup sugar
1 egg yolk

1 large tablespoon heavy cream
3½ cups white flour
Dash of almond extract

Cream sugar and butter until very creamy and white in color. Stir in egg yolk, cream and almond extract. Work in flour until dough is a consistency that it can be pressed into tins. Bake until light brown in 400° oven — 10-12 minutes. Watch carefully. Makes approximately four dozen cookies.

Sandkaker tins are 2½ inches in diameter and ¾-inch deep, with corrugated sides. Can be purchased in most stores carrying imported ware. If not available, one might experiment with muffin tins, though there is no guarantee that they will be satisfactory!

THE LEMON FILLING

5 tablespoons cornstarch
1 cup white sugar
2 cups boiling water
2 well-beaten egg yolks

2 tablespoons butter
Juice of 2 lemons
Grated rind of 1 lemon
Pinch of salt

Mix well cornstarch and sugar. Pour in boiling water. Stir well and boil for about 10 minutes, stirring constantly so no lumps form. Lift off fire and add egg yolks and butter. Heat again until eggs are set. Cool a little; add lemon juice, rind and salt. Stir well.

THE MERINGUE

2 egg whites   5 tablespoons sugar
A bit of lemon juice

Beat egg whites until stiff. Add lemon juice and sugar gradually. Keep beating until meringue stands in peaks.

THE ASSEMBLING

Fill *sandkaker* with lemon filling. Top with meringue. Brown in slow oven, 300-350°.

This portion of filling is enough for about 25.

Mrs. Florea's Banana Cake!

By JUDITH LINDQUIST

It had been a busy Sunday afternoon, the opening session of the Trumbull Baptist Association annual meeting. Our speaker was none other than Mrs. Howard G. Colwell, who thrilled our hearts with her inspiring message. We wanted her to visit our Campbell Christian Center before she left that evening. Two carloads of folks paused at Neighborhood House and then we came down to Bethel House where we were planning to build a bit of fellowship about a cup of coffee. We knew that Mrs. Florea had baked a delicious banana cake so we were sure we could "borrow" something good from her apartment.

Perhaps I should tell you a bit about Mrs. Florea. She has an apartment in Bethel House where the missionaries live. She cleans the building, but she does a great deal more. She has a continuous song of praise for her Lord! Through her oldest daughter she was won to the Lord a number of years ago and she never tires of telling how happy she is as a Christian. Her prayers rise "night and day" for those who do not know Him as their personal Savior. And she not only prays for them, she goes out to seek them, always with a testimony!

Mrs. Florea also is a good cook. So back to banana cake! The coffee was done, the table was set, and we went to look for the cake. (We knew she would not be cross because she always has told us to help ourselves to her cakes.) Alas and alack! During the day she had had some company, and the cake was gone — all but a small piece. So each of us had a piece about the size of those slices of wedding cake we used to get before they began making such huge ones. We filled in with our old stand-by, crackers and cheese. But we had a good time just the same.

It reminded us of the other time, when we had helped ourselves to Mrs. Florea's cake, and her daughter came for a visit, her mouth "watering" for a piece of "mother's banana cake." It was gone that time, too!

OHIO

137

BANANA CAKE

2 cups flour
1 cup sugar
2 bananas
1 teaspoon vanilla
Pinch of salt
2 tablespoons baking powder

Pinch baking soda
1 cup milk
¾ cup Crisco or other shortening
3 eggs—separate yolk and white

Cream sugar and shortening; sift flour, baking powder, soda, salt. Mix with sugar and shortening. Grate bananas and put into mixture. Put in beaten yolks of eggs. Add milk gradually (you may not need all of it). Fold in whites of eggs well beaten and put in pan for baking.

PIGS IN BLANKETS

SERVED AT BETHEL FIRST AID CLASS PARTY

Mix well: ½ pound pork, ½ pound beef, 2 small onions, cut fine, 1 egg, and salt and pepper. Put a little grease in skillet with some onion, cut fine, a little water and about ¾ cup rice. Fry the rice till it is brown. Let it cool and mix with meat. Put head of cabbage in hot water, almost boiling, for about ten minutes, and leaves will come off easily. Put one or more tablespoons of the meat and rice mixture on a cabbage leaf, and wrap the leaf around the mixture. Use toothpicks to hold it together. Put in pot with about 1 can of sauerkraut and a little water. Cook slowly until done, a little more than one hour.

When the Sky Darkened

By JUDITH LINDQUIST

No matter when we eat these cookies I always think of our dear friend, Mrs. P. She makes them so that they fairly melt in your mouth. We had some the day we were invited to her house. You remember, the day when it became so dark in the middle of the afternoon?

For some time Mrs. P. planned to invite the missionaries for dinner when her husband could be at home, too. So we were invited for Sunday dinner. On Saturday she made most of her preparations so she would not have to miss church the next morning.

Coming to church for morning worship is very much a part of her life now, but there was a time when Mrs. P. did not care much for it. Later came a time of searching of her heart. She wanted to become a Christian. With the prayerful help of another dear Christian, she was won to Christ. Then she wanted to be baptized, but she thought her husband would raise many objections. She was almost afraid to be baptized. But finally one day she took the step. In fear and trembling she faced her husband. But the Lord was working on his heart, too.

A while later, her husband was laid aside by illness. He had time to think. His daughter, a Christian nurse, helped to take care of him. His wife had time for quiet talks with him, too. During that period of illness, he came to an understanding with the Lord and he, too, felt the desire to tell to everyone that he was a Christian. It made us all very happy when on Palm Sunday he went down into the baptismal waters with the words on his lips, "Praise the Lord!"

We richly enjoyed the dinner in that Christian home. We had just finished eating when we looked out to find that the sky was orange colored. It seemed queer. We thought a big storm must be coming. After we washed the dishes, we sat down to await the storm which never came. But it grew darker and darker, truly uncanny. People came with all kinds of rumors about the cause of it, but still we sat in the peculiar darkness. Finally it lifted. How much the fellowship with calm Christians meant during that eerie hour!

OHIO

139

Crazy Cake

By HAZEL N. PENN

The Methodist parsonage needed paint! But paint was expensive and painters scarce. The men in the church decided to do more than give enough money to buy paint. They arranged to give time to do the work themselves. One who was a painter was naturally recognized as the director of the project.

All morning they painted and accomplished a great deal. What appetites they had when noon and dinnertime arrived!

The women prepared a basket dinner and served it at the church. I made a Crazy Cake just before noon and took it over for dessert. Everyone liked it. Several men praised it. As a result I was swamped with requests for my recipe.

OHIO

CRAZY CAKE

1 cup granulated sugar	1 teaspoon vanilla
1½ cups cake flour	1 teaspoon vinegar
⅓ cup cocoa	⅓ cup salad oil
1 teaspoon soda	½ teaspoon salt

Blend dry ingredients thoroughly. Sift. With batter spoon make three holes in the blended materials. In one, put 1 teaspoon vanilla; in another put 1 teaspoon vinegar; in the other, put ⅓ cup of any brand of salad oil. Mix lightly with spoon. Then add 1 cup cold water. Beat well with electric beater. Pour into ungreased pan (about 8 x 10 in size). The batter is very thin before cake is baked. Bake at 350°, 30 minutes.

This cake is good frosted with a cocoa and powdered sugar topping or boiled seven-minute frosting.

Vitamins and Virtue

By RUTH L. GILBERT

Two Comanche Indian boys were setting up camp at a work project. While the missionary talked with the parents, the missionary's wife chatted with the boys. This was the first time the younger one had ever camped away from the parents.

Tragedy struck that night in the form of a cold, driving rain that sent the older boy to the hospital with pneumonia. A few days later he died, and again the missionary's wife talked with the younger one, this time to give him God's word of comfort and consolation.

Occasionally the boy ate at the missionary's table, and after a time became quite regular at the prayer meetings. This being the only form of social activity for Christian people, cake and coffee are served after the prayer service, and all stay and visit for a while.

One Sunday the Comanche boy said to the missionary's wife, "I'm not going to the prayer meeting this time." Knowing the outside pull that draws young men away from church, she said, "Oh, you'd better come. I'll make a chocolate cake just for you!"

The cake was made. The lad was there to eat it and to sing a sacred solo. The missionary rejoiced as she saw him with his chocolate cake, mingling with Godly people, laughing quietly and enjoying the fellowship — free from the danger and temptations of the town streets.

OKLAHOMA

CHOCOLATE CAKE

2 cups flour	$\frac{1}{2}$ teaspoon salt
$\frac{1}{2}$ cup cocoa	2 egg yolks
1 cup sugar	$1\frac{1}{4}$ cups sour milk
1 teaspoon soda	$\frac{1}{4}$ cup melted shortening
2 teaspoons baking powder	1 teaspoon vanilla

2 egg whites, stiff

Sift dry ingredients four times. Add sour milk and egg yolks, and stir or beat till smooth. Add vanilla and shortening. Fold in beaten whites of eggs. Bake in greased pan, 35 or 40 minutes. Oven: 375°.

FROSTING: Mix thoroughly $\frac{1}{2}$ cup sugar and $\frac{1}{4}$ cup cocoa. Add 6 teaspoons water and cream. Place over fire and stir till smooth and glossy (about 3 minutes). Add butter the size of a pecan, and 1 teaspoon vanilla. Blend and spread.

141

Good Lemon Flavor

By Alice C. Lorimer

We live near a university. Realizing how good it seems to college folks to "get one's feet under a table in a home," we invited one of the college boys to share our evening meal. It was good to watch his pleasure as he tasted the various foods served to him. But when it came time for the dessert! He ate several mouthfuls, held his spoon aloft, all but smacked his lips, looked at me and said, "What is it?"

This recipe was sent to me by a relative in New York. When you want something extra special, try it — that is, if you like that real lemon flavor, the kind that has a tang to it.

Vermont

LEMON SPONGE PUDDING

1 cup sugar	2 egg yolks
2 tablespoons flour	1 cup milk
2 tablespoons butter	2 egg whites, beaten
Juice and rind of one lemon	

Cream butter, sugar and flour together. Add milk to beaten egg yolks and add to other ingredients. Add lemon juice and rind. Fold in beaten egg whites. Pour in greased baking dish, set in pan of hot water. Bake 45 minutes to 1 hour in moderate oven.

To make it de luxe, top with whipped cream, cherries or nuts.

Chinese Style—Seattle

By Mildred L. Cummings

It was just a family dinner to which I was invited by the Yook family of Seattle, Washington. There were Mr. and Mrs. Yook and their four sturdy children. While waiting for dinner four-year-old Thomas entertained me by playing several "pieces" on the piano. Mr. Yook did most of the cooking that night and what a delightful meal it was. Hands were joined around the table as one of the children expressed gratitude to God for the food.

Our dinner was prepared in Chinese style. We had spareribs, rice, roast pork, green vegetable cooked with meat, vegetable soup, delicious tea and kumquats.

Mrs. Yook was attending classes at the university and since has secured a position in the public school system as a kindergarten teacher — the only Chinese in the system!

CALIFORNIA

SPARERIBS—CHINESE STYLE

2½ or 3 pounds spareribs, cut in one inch pieces. Season with salt and pepper and fry brown. Pour off grease.

Add water and cook about an hour. Take meat out and make gravy.

GRAVY:

1 cup soy sauce
1 cup white or brown sugar
1 heaping teaspoon cornstarch

1 cup pineapple juice or small pieces of pineapple
½ cup water

Stir until it boils then pour over meat. Serve with rice.

RICE—CHINESE STYLE

Wash rice about six times, rubbing in hands to get off outside husks. Add cold water to one inch above rice. Put on tight cover and do not remove while cooking. High fire until it boils, then reduce heat to low. Cook about 40 minutes.

Home
Away from Home Party

By FLORENCE STANSBURY

It was nine-thirty New Year's Eve. The punch bowl was full of good rich creamy eggnog, and the plates were filled with sandwiches, fruit cake, fruit, cheese and crackers. Just in time, too, for the first guest was arriving.

Our New Year's party is an occasion for friends who are away from family and loved ones to be together for an evening of fun and Christian fellowship. From India, China, Japan, the Philippine Islands and Latin America they come to enrich our fellowship and deepen our understanding of the Christian world family.

Friends from around the world vie with each other in the telling of family traditions and holiday customs in celebrating the birthday of the Savior. Games, singing and stunts make us one happy group.

The time for food is always fun. We try to serve as the *piece de resistance* a dish of another country. On this special night it was Haitian Salad which we had enjoyed with missionaries in Haiti several years before.

Half an hour before the midnight bells and whistles began, our group began to talk over together some dreams for the new year. One friend expressed the hope that she might more fully live the meaning of the song of her people, "Lord, I want to be more loving in my heart." Another was anxious to get back to India to put into practice so many of the new insights he had as the result of his study.

Still another recalled a poem she had read calling upon all to remember that men are brothers whatever their name, and that which lifts one helps all.

Another friend shared a letter that had come to her from a family in France. The man of the house needed shoes, large size, and the children needed warm clothes. Needs that were later filled by the friends.

As the midnight whistles and bells began to sound through the cold night, our group was led in prayer. During these moments full of rich fellowship we were bound even more closely together in the bonds of Christian love and brotherhood!

To us the words "Happy New Year" had new meaning as our friends reluctantly donned coats, hats and galoshes. It had been an evening we shall always remember!

NEW YORK

HAITIAN SALAD

8 cups shrimp, cleaned and diced	3 cups avocado
2 cups blanched almonds	4 cups halved Tokay grapes
3 cups diced celery	3 cups chopped hard-boiled eggs

Dice avocado into lemon juice to preserve color. Drain before adding to other ingredients. Place all ingredients in large mixing bowl. Salt and pepper to taste. Mix ingredients together, blending lightly with boiled dressing. The amount of dressing needed depends upon how moist you like your salad. I don't like it very moist, so about 4 cups are enough for me!

Serves 25 to 30 people.

BOILED DRESSING

2 tablespoons flour	2 tablespoons milk for paste
1 tablespoon sugar	1 egg
½ teaspoon salt	1 tablespoon butter
Dash of pepper	1 cup milk
½ cup white vinegar	

Mix together thoroughly: flour, sugar, salt, pepper. Add enough milk to make smooth, thin paste. Pour this into 1 cup of milk. Beat egg until it is light and frothy. Add egg to mixture. Blend well. Put this into a saucepan and cook over a very slow fire. Stir constantly. As this begins to thicken, add the vinegar slowly—almost drop by drop. Stir all the time. Blend in butter just before taking from the fire.

CREAMY EGGNOG

2 quarts milk	4 tablespoons cinnamon
1 quart heavy cream	4 teaspoons nutmeg
16 egg yolks whipped until lemon color	2 teaspoons cloves
8 egg whites beaten until frothy	2 teaspoons salt
8 egg whites—hold for later use	1 cup sugar
	¾ cup vanilla

In one bowl or pitcher place milk. In second bowl place cinnamon, clove, nutmeg, salt and sugar. Mix dry ingredients together thoroughly. To the dry ingredients add slowly enough milk to dissolve them completely. Now add egg yolks. Stir well. Add this mixture to milk, blending thoroughly. Pour in cream and frothy egg white. Stir until all ingredients are blended. Let stand for 24 hours, stirring occasionally.

When ready to serve, pour eggnog into punch bowl. Whip remaining egg whites until they are dry and stiff. Float on top of eggnog. Serves about 20 people. Be sure to make plenty. This will disappear in a hurry!

The Announcement Party

By Dorothy A. Stevens

Today was the announcement party for Doris and Judson!

Florence came home on Sunday. Monday, we ordered supplies and polished silver; Tuesday, we cleaned and cleaned; Wednesday, we made our creamy rich eggnog and sandwiches for seventy-five people and finished last-minute decorations and went to Watch Night service at our church. Today, New Year's Day, was the party. But with the holiday also came an influenza epidemic and icy rain to sheathe the highways, to say nothing of the bus strike!

Doris was due at 10:15 by train, but Judson was driving in! Such excitement! Both arrived safely, but we had word from Long Island and New Jersey that the roads were glazed or that "flu" had struck. Would anyone be able to get to our home when there were so many hazards?

"At home from four until seven o'clock." However, the first guests arrived about three and the last left about eleven, and at least sixty signed the ANNOUNCEMENT page of the Bride's Book.

Doris and Judson are both in Christian work. She is a state director and he is a pastor in Ohio. So we invited them to New York to greet their many friends here. National church leaders, local church friends, business people, radio and television personalities, members of the family, and children out for afternoon fun. A good cross-section of American Christian "home folks"!

The bride- and groom-to-be are choice spirits and glowed happily in the midst of their friends. Corsages for the hostesses and bunch after bunch of red roses, from friends far and near, made a colorful background for true happiness.

In the midst of cheery chatter, one guest whispered to his hostess the only thing that could have made the day more wonderful. It was too good to keep, so all were called to attention and it was announced that the last four Baptist missionaries, held in solitary house confinement for many, many months, were arriving in Hong Kong by January second, this same day on the other side of the world! What rejoicing over this good news, too; and then a precious prayer of thanksgiving. Two items of good news told in our home on that same day: Doris and Judson in their happiness, and The Four free at last! Our home had been blessed once more by grace and joy.

Rarified happiness does not fill the inner man, however. But spicy, creamy eggnog and hundreds of sandwiches and chicken salad *and* Mrs. Stansbury's homemade fruitcake — ten pounds of it for the joyful occasion — rounded out, shall we say, the hospitality of our announcement party.

NEW YORK

PARTY FARE

MARBLE SANDWICHES

Three thin slices of sandwich-type white bread and two of whole wheat make five or six sandwiches. Lay on sandwich board, alternating white and dark bread. Butter—or margarine—one side of four slices. Cover other side of dark slices with pink pimento cheese spread and other side of two white with pineapple cheese spread—one white slice has NO butter on it. Stack: white, dark, white, dark, white. Using a very sharp breadknife, remove crusts and slice evenly into five or six sandwiches—striped with bread and with filling. Wrap immediately in wax paper; be sure sandwiches are kept straight at edges and do not press together. Four packages—20 or 24 sandwiches will fit into a bread-loaf wrapper. Sandwiches keep in refrigerator for twenty-four hours.

WATER CRESS SANDWICHES

Cut wax paper twice as long and 2½ times as wide as a slice of bread. Prepare these strips of paper in advance. Wash and select choice branches of watercress. Remove all crusts from slice of bread. Butter one end of the slice heavily for about one inch, and spread the remainder of that side with mayonnaise. Lay bread on strip with butter end away from you. Place watercress on end toward you, with some leaves sticking beyond edge of bread. Place little fingers at end of bread away from you; pick up strip-end toward you, and curve bread over watercress, using strip to support bread. Pull strip tight as end folds over, and continue to roll bread. Twist ends of strip to hold roll in shape. Butter will do that after sandwich is chilled. Place five sandwich rolls together in loaf-wrapper. Room for ten. Sandwiches will keep fresh for twenty-four hours in a cold place.

CHICKEN SALAD

4 cups chicken—diced	2 cups celery—diced
2 cups avocado—diced	2 cups mayonnaise
2 cups hard-boiled eggs—diced	2 cups pecan meats
1 lemon	Salt and pepper to taste

We use Richardson and Robbins canned chicken. Two cans make four heaping cups. Squeeze juice of one lemon in ½ cup of water. Bathe avocado in lemon juice as rapidly as it is peeled. This keeps it from turning brown. Let stand for 5 minutes. Stir chicken, avocado, eggs and celery with one cup of mayonnaise. Cover and chill in refrigerator. When ready to serve, add second cup of mayonnaise and nut meats. Mix thoroughly. Serve on lettuce leaves. About 18 helpings.

MRS. STANSBURY'S FRUITCAKE

Cream together 1 cup sugar, ½ cup Crisco, ½ teaspoon each of salt, nutmeg, cinnamon and cloves. Dissolve 1 teaspoon soda and 2 teaspoons baking powder in a little hot water and pour over 1 cup applesauce. Dredge (dust lightly with flour) 1 cup each of raisins, chopped candied fruits and chopped nut meats. Add fruit and nuts to applesauce. Stir into this mixture 1¾ cups flour. Add creamed sugar. Crisco and spices. Pour into loaf pan and bake one hour at 350°.

149

Some Favorite Recipes

By DOROTHY A. STEVENS

MY MOTHER'S FRUIT SALAD

½ pound malaga grapes
1 can sliced pineapple

1 bunch celery
¼ pound almonds

Use silver knife. Cut pineapple in cubes; cut grapes into halves and seed; cut celery into small pieces. Mix grapes and pineapple in colander. Set on ice to drain. Place celery in cold water until ready to use. Blanche almonds and put in ice water until ready to use.

DRESSING: ¼ cup cream—whipped after measuring; 2 tablespoons lemon juice; 1 teaspoon granulated sugar; 1 pinch red pepper. Mix together.

When ready to serve, toss fruit, nuts and celery together in a large platter; pour dressing over, and serve on lettuce leaves. 8 portions.

PLUM NUTTY

5 pounds large blue plums
5 pounds sugar

2 oranges
1 pound pecan nut meats

Cut plums in half and remove pits. Cook in boiler with just enough water to keep plums from burning. Put half sugar in immediately. Add the rest of the sugar as the first melts. Add the juice of two oranges and the rind of one when the conserve is nearly done. Boil until quite thick, but not ready to jell. Add pecans and stir them in after the Plum Nutty comes off the stove. Fill jars, but do not cap until cool. This is a very old recipe.

We sometimes take two large cans of purple plums, remove the pits and put in boiler to cook. When syrup gets thick, add juice of one orange and half the rind. Cook until thick but not ready to jell. Remove from stove and stir in a quarter of a pound of pecan nut meats. Put in jars and cap when cool. This makes a rich and pungent conserve.

SPICED TEA PUNCH

18 cups sugar
9 cups water
18 cups tea infusion
10 cups orange juice
6 cups grapefruit juice

6 cups lemon juice
4 cups pineapple juice
4 cups cinnamon juice
4 cups clove juice
8 quarts orange sherbet

12 cups infusion—orange, lemon and grapefruit rind

Make syrup of sugar and water. Make tea infusion by pouring boiling water over tea leaves, a tablespoon of tea to each cup. Make juice by pouring boiling water over spices, a tablespoon of spice to a cup of water. Strain juices and tea separately. Make early and keep in separate containers in refrigerator until ready to serve. Submerge orange, lemon and grapefruit halves in water and boil slowly until rinds are soft. Strain off juice, bottle and keep in cool place until ready to serve. When ready to serve, all syrup and juices may be mixed in one large container, or proportionate parts may be mixed at a time. Put two or three quart bricks of orange sherbet in punch bowl instead of regular ice. Pour mixture over sherbet. Allow to stand for about one hour before serving. Sherbet enriches, does not dilute the punch. 100 servings.

SUET PUDDING

EDNA S. STANTON'S GRANDMOTHER'S RECIPE

2 eggs	1 teaspoon salt
1 cup milk	2 teaspoons baking powder,
1 cup molasses	sifted in
½ cup suet, chopped fine	3 short cups flour

1 teaspoon each: cloves, cinnamon, nutmeg

As much fruit, stoned raisins and citron as you like. To make pudding lighter, use butter instead of suet. Mix ingredients together. Steam for two hours.

SPECIALTY SALAD

EDNA KEMPER, COLORADO

Soak 1 tablespoon gelatine in 2 tablespoons cold water. Beat 2 eggs well, and add to 4 tablespoons of sugar and 4 tablespoons of vinegar. Put in double boiler and beat while cooking. Add gelatine and 2 tablespoons of butter. Remove from fire and cool. Add 2 cups pitted sweet cherries; 2 cups pineapple, cut into bites, 1 cup orange sections. Fold in 1 cup cream, whipped. Pour into mold and put in refrigerator for 12 hours. Serves 6 to 8. Very good.

151

Indices

Contributors

Recipes

154

THE AMERICAS—NORTH AMERICA

Types of Food

Table Talk and Tidbits

Stevens, Dorothy A. Edited